A WINTERTHUR GUIDE TO
AMERICAN NEEDLEWORK

WINTERTHUR

A WINTERTHUR GUIDE TO
AMERICAN NEEDLEWORK

Susan Burrows Swan

Susan Burrows Swan

A Winterthur Book/Rutledge Books
Crown Publishers, Inc.

Cover Illustration: Plate XI.

Abbreviations Used in the Captions:

acc. no. = accession number
cm = centimeters
H = height
L = length
W = width

Copyright © 1976 The Henry Francis du Pont Winterthur Museum.
All rights reserved, including the right of reproduction in
whole or in part.
Prepared and produced by Rutledge Books, a division of Arcata
Consumer Products Corporation, 25 West 43 Street, New York,
N.Y. 10036.
Published by Crown Publishers, Inc., One Park Avenue, New York,
N.Y. 10016. Published simultaneously in Canada by General
Publishing Company, Ltd.
First printing 1976
Printed in the United States of America

Library of Congress Cataloging in Publication Data
Swan, Susan Burrows.
  A Winterthur guide to American needlework.

  (A Winterthur book/Rutledge books)
  Bibliography: p. 142.
  1. Needlework—United States. 2. Henry
Francis du Pont Winterthur Museum. I. Henry
Francis du Pont Winterthur Museum. II. Title.
NK8812.595 1976   746.4′4   76-10602
ISBN 0-517-52177-6 paper
ISBN 0-517-52785-5 cloth

Contents

Introduction

This guide presents 117 representative examples of the American needlework contained in the Henry Francis du Pont Winterthur Museum. The major needlework techniques used in America, the dates of their popularity, and the stitches used to execute them are briefly described. Whenever possible, terms familiar to our ancestors have been used to describe forms, techniques, and stitches.

Almost from the time that he began his great collection of Americana, Henry Francis du Pont acquired needlework. As he became involved in assembling room settings that were compatible with the early furniture they were to display, he recognized the necessity of acquiring appropriate accessories. The result was a growing needlework collection, embracing an ever-broadening spectrum of techniques. By the time the museum opened to the public in 1951, Mr. du Pont had created one of the outstanding needlework and needlework tool collections in the country (Figure 1). The collection has continued to grow, and today it contains more than six hundred examples of American needlework, ranging in date from 1680 to 1880.

It is fortunate that Mr. du Pont recognized so early the importance of needlework in the early American home, for the needle arts were women's major contribution to the decorative arts in the preindustrial era.

Needlework, and textiles generally, were accorded high monetary value and were therefore far more important to the colonial American family than they are to its counterpart today. Contemporary wills and inventories, in which possessions were often listed in the order of their importance, give evidence of this. After land, money, and silverware came household textiles, clothing, and needlework. Towels, sheets, articles of clothing—even undergarments—were considered worth mentioning. Most clothing was

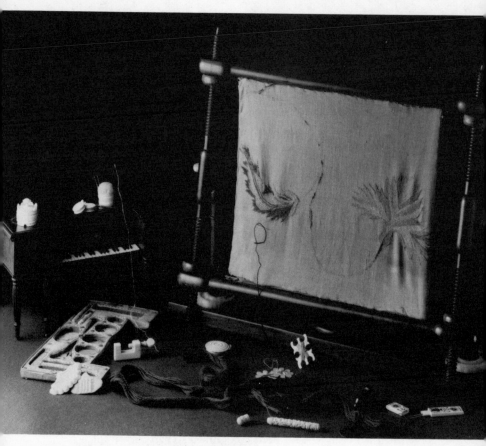

Figure 1. Left: *Piano-shaped sewing and music box of inlaid mahogany. English; 1800–25; H. 6¾″ (17.14 cm), L. 12⁷/₁₆″ (31.59 cm); acc. no. 61.1026. Right: Adjustable needlework frame made of cherry and walnut with ivory and alabaster trim. 1800–40; H. 19⅛″ (48.59 cm), W. 23″ (58.42 cm); acc. no. 58.2974.*

Figure 1

8

worn, mended, remodeled, redyed, and then passed to the next generation where the process might be repeated. Needlework items received special attention in the inventories because of the personal associations they represented. Accordingly, they were treasured beyond their basic monetary value as textiles.

Three distinct classifications of needlework existed in the eighteenth century, as revealed in newspaper advertisements, diaries, and journals: *plain sewing*, *marking*, and *fancy work*. Plain sewing referred to hemming, seaming, and the construction of simple garments such as nightgowns and aprons. Knitting also seems to have been considered plain work. To keep accurate account of household linens and clothing, each piece was marked with cross-stitched initials, numbers, or dates. Fancy needlework consisted of all other forms of embroidery, including tambour, crewel, and canvas work. It was considered essential for every woman to have a knowledge of plain sewing and, usually, marking. Fancy needlework, however, was usually reserved for the more privileged, those girls whose parents could afford to send them to embroidery school.

In many cases, the stitches used in fancy needlework were known by several names, and those names changed as time passed. In my research, I enjoy discovering original terminology as found in inventories, wills, newspapers, letters, and diaries. Most of these terms were so familiar to our ancestors that there was no need to explain them. Although it is fascinating to study the evolution of needlework terminology, my ultimate interest is in the women who created the needlework and their role in society—a subject I hope to explore in detail in another book.

I have discovered a sharing and adventurous spirit among colleagues and friends, many of whom have given me references that they thought might prove useful in my research for this guide. To those many thoughtful people, I give grateful thanks. My most ardent appreciation goes to my husband, whose aid and support have been invaluable.

Samplers

As embroidery forms, probably more samplers have survived than any other type of American needlework. They were heirlooms, preserved from one generation to the next. Today it is common but inaccurate to consider any piece of embroidery that bears a name and a date to be a sampler, for, by this definition, some bed hangings, pocketbooks, tablecloths, and many pictures would be classified as samplers. A more workable description includes only needlework intended to record stitches and designs, to serve either as a sort of reference notebook or as a "sample" statement of ability. Some needlework, clearly intended for this purpose, lacks dates and even names.

A variety of fineness is found in the background fabrics used for samplers. Linen cloth was the most common backing, although wool and cotton—alone or in combination—are occasionally found. A few samplers, especially those made in the nineteenth century, were done on canvas. Most samplers were embroidered in silk or linen thread on plain-woven linen. Far less common today, in part owing to the work of moths, are samplers worked with crewel (worsted) yarns (Figure 2). By 1830, however, the soft Berlin wool yarns had invaded the sampler field. Like the crewel yarns, many of these retain their vivid colors, but because they were of a heavier denier, they appear coarser than the worsteds.

The size, shape, and design of the sampler, as well as the intention of and the age at which the embroiderer worked her piece, changed over the years of American sampler making. The few existing seventeenth- and early eighteenth-century samplers are long (fifteen to thirty inches) and narrow (six to eight inches). These early samplers, usually worked by women fifteen years old or older, served primarily to record stitches and designs. Rolled when not in use, unrolled when needed to recall a pattern or stitch, they were not intended for framing. They consisted of bands of embroidery, lace, canvas-work designs, or combinations of these techniques (Plate I). Some appear to be unfinished, for the em-

Figure 2

Figure 2. *Sampler of crewel yarns on linen showing three bands of designs, alphabets, and a verse: "Jane Simon her sampler made In the Tenth Year of her Age • 1737 • The Graciovs God Did Give Me Time To Do Ths Work You See that Others Mayd Larn The Same When I Shall Cease to Be." Cross, eyelet, satin, back, and Irish stitches; experimental drawn work with linen thread near a tulip. History of ownership in Oyster Bay, Long Island; H. 20¹⁵⁄₁₆″ (53.18 cm), W. 8⁵⁄₁₆″ (21.20 cm); acc. no. 75.40.*

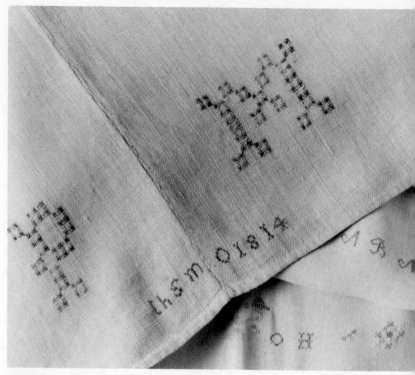

Figure 3

Figure 3. *Top: Sheet marked in cross-stitched block initials "PM" in pink and blue and "th 5 mo 1814" in smaller blue letters; acc. no. 67.753. Center: Pillowcase with cross-stitched script initials "AB No 11." Ca. 1800; gift of Mr. and Mrs. Charles F. Montgomery; acc. no. 59.1.4. Bottom: Sheet with stylized flowers and block initials "OH." Ca. 1800; acc. no. 60.1122.*

broiderer would reserve spaces in which to add new bands of stitching as she acquired new skills or designs. She did not start with a preconceived total design. These early samplers also displayed alphabets and numerals; some included verses.

Early in the eighteenth century, girls between the ages of five and twelve began to make samplers. The primary purpose of these samplers was to provide practice in working numerals and alphabets. The same letters and numerals recorded on these samplers were then copied onto clóthing and household linens, for "proper" housekeeping required that all clothing and household linens be marked. The simplest form of marking called for working the initials in cross stitch, but sometimes marking involved the use of whole names, dates, and a separate identification number for each item (Figure 3). Some samplers include in their text the word *marked* or *markt*, thus disproving the modern assumption that samplers were used as tools in the learning of reading or writing. A single sampler might contain as many as eight styles of letters together with several different sets of numerals.

As the eighteenth century progressed, many young girls began to add pictorial elements to their numerals and alphabets. Dated samplers demonstrate a gradual shift in emphasis from recording stitches and patterns toward creating more decorative pictorial designs. By the mid-eighteenth century, not only were samplers pictorial, they also more closely approached a square in overall shape. Borders were added, small at first, later becoming more prominent (Figures 4 and 5). In *Reminiscences of a Nonagenarian*, Sarah Anna Emery, writing about the early nineteenth century, said, "Every girl was taught to embroider letters in marking stitch. One was considered very poorly educated who could not exhibit a sampler; some of these were large and elaborate specimens of handiwork; framed and glazed, they often formed the chief ornament of the sitting room or best parlor."

Advertisements of framers, accounts of cabinetmakers, and the labels occasionally found pasted on the backs of frames attest to the practice of framing needlework. For instance, Thomas Ellis, a glazier, announced in the *Pennsylvania Journal* of May 17,

1750, that he sold "London Crown [glass] of any size for Clocks, Samplers, Pictures, &c."

As schooling for girls became increasingly common throughout the eighteenth and nineteenth centuries, the production of samplers increased proportionately, for most samplers were probably made in schools. Many of those that survive record the first attempts at a simple alphabet by five-year-old girls attending a dame school. Others, worked by fifteen- or sixteen-year-old girls as a final piece at an academy, display more sophisticated renderings. Some schools developed distinctive sampler designs; as a result, some samplers are easily traced to a particular school (Plate II; Figures 6 and 7).

After 1800, certain specialized sampler forms became more prevalent. One such form was called *family records* or *genealogy*. Some of these present a family tree (Figure 8); others, less inventive, merely list in chart form the names, dates of births, and dates of deaths in the needleworker's family. Dates of subsequent marriages and deaths were sometimes added later.

Figure 4

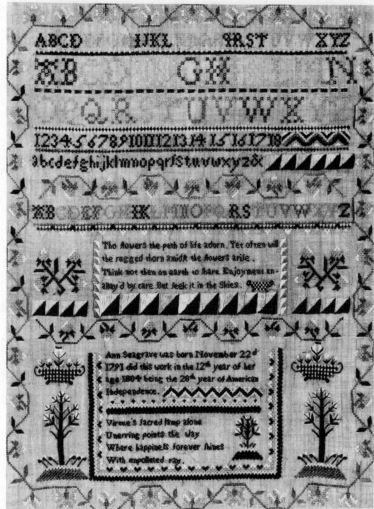

Figure 5

Figure 4. *Almost square sampler of linen with bright polychrome silk embroidery in cross, satin, back, outline, eyelet, and poorly done bullion stitches. Reading, Mass.; H. 15⅛" (38.43 cm), W. 15¼" (38.73 cm); acc. no. 63.515.* **Figure 5.** *Sampler of natural linen ground with polychrome silk embroidery in cross, Queen's, eyelet, tent, and satin stitches. H. 22⅛" (56.21 cm), W. 17" (43.18 cm); Odessa Properties, Winterthur Museum; gift of H. Rodney Sharp; acc. no. 59.3722.*

15

Figure 6

Figure 6. *Wide-bordered sampler divided into segments on very fine linen with brightly colored silk yarns, possibly made as a present for a teacher. The verse begins "Leah Gallagher and Rachel Armstrong the Daughters of George and Sarah Bratten Was born at one birth near Wilmington [Del.],"* tells of their baptism and marriages, then, "opened School in Lancaster on the First day of May 1792 and had this sampler made by one of her scholars viz Sarah Holsworth in the year of our LORD 1799." The building with birds roosting on its roof is the Lancaster County Poorhouse. Stitches are cross, tent, satin, back, chain, outline, eyelet, and Queen's. Notice how the threads are carried from word to word. Pennsylvania; H. 17" (43.18 cm); W. 16½" (41.91 cm); acc. no. 57.671.

Figure 7. *As an orphan, Mary Pennell Corbit was cared for by her uncle, William Corbit, who lived in Appoquinimink, now Odessa, Del. Mary worked this typical Friends school design, with scattered initials representing her relatives, when she was 11. Her uncle's account book lists a "gilt frame for sampler" purchased in Wilmington, presumably for this piece, on May 14, 1823. Linen with beige, brown, and blue cross-stitch embroidery. H. 15¾" (40 cm), W. 15¼" (38.73 cm); Odessa Properties, Winterthur Museum; acc. no. 71.1525.*

Figure 7

16

Figure 8

Figure 8. *Genealogical tree sampler with family names stitched on the yellow fruit; at least four others are known from the Concord-Lexington area. This one was worked by Lorenza Fisk with the last date 1811; stitches are satin, outline, tent, flat, cross, and chain. H. 19¼" (48.89 cm), W. 16½" (41.91 cm); gift of Mrs. Alfred C. Harrison; acc. no. 69.430.*

Figure 9. *Darning sampler on white plain-woven linen with darning stitches in white cotton yarns. Name in black silk cross stitch. Dated 1820. H. 8⅛″ (20.65 cm), W. 8¾″ (22.22 cm); acc. no. 69.771.*

Figure 9

Another specialized form of sampler was the darning sampler, which demonstrated the practice of invisible mending (Figure 9). During an age that found fabrics so expensive that most clothing was worn to shreds, the darning sampler provided a sensible way to teach girls a very necessary skill. To make such a sampler, a piece of cloth was cut to simulate a tear—both straight cuts and L-shaped cuts were used—and then rewoven with yarns in a contrasting color or texture, to facilitate later study and recall by the darner.

The very few surviving lacework samplers represent one of the loveliest expressions of the needle arts taught in the eighteenth century. Frances Paschal demonstrated two kinds of lacework (Figure 10). She used cutwork for the circles and the narrow rectangle surrounding her name; to fashion the lacy leaves, she used Dresden work, the term by which drawn work was known in the eighteenth century.

In cutwork, the needlewoman worked the edges of the design

Figure 10

Figure 10. *Lacework sampler on plain-woven cotton and linen ground. Corner circles and rectangle are done in cutwork, flowers and leaves in drawn, or Dresden, work, stems in chain stitch; flowers are edged with satin, chain, and buttonhole stitches worked in linen thread. H. 8″ (20.32 cm), W. 9¼″ (23.49 cm); acc. no. 59.89*

Figure 11. *Long white apron made of finely woven combination of cotton and linen, with white drawn or Dresden work in small circle decorations. 1760–1810; L. 32⁹/₁₆″ (82.70 cm), W. 29⁵/₈″ (75.26 cm); Odessa Properties, Winterthur Museum; acc. no. 71.1284.*

Figure 11

elements in chain, buttonhole, or satin stitch to prevent the raveling of the fabric. Then she carefully cut away the background fabric inside the stitching lines. Repeated rows of buttonhole stitches created needle-made lace to refill the empty areas. Another variation of cutwork starts with radiating lines resembling a spiderweb. Martha Logan advertised in the *South Carolina Gazette* (Charleston) of March 27–April 3, 1742, her willingness to teach cutwork.

To fashion design elements in Dresden work, the needleworker carefully cut away several warp or weft threads and then embroidered the remaining threads together to complete the pattern. Sometimes, because of the very fine backgrounds in Dresden work, no threads were removed; they were simply pulled together

Figure 12

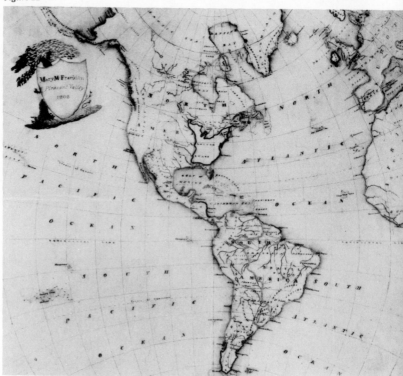

Figure 13

Figure 12. *Mary M. Franklin, of Pleasant Valley, N.Y., made this map sampler in 1808. The background is lightweight, plain-woven white silk with the continents outlined in black silk chenille yarns; the tree behind the shield is green and brown chenille; rivers are black silk thread; water near the coastline is painted blue; names are stitched or drawn in black ink, and the longitudinal lines are also drawn in ink. Several similar examples are known. H. 20⅜″ (51.76 cm), W. 23¾″ (60.32 cm); acc. no. 57.552.* **Figure 13.** *Globe sampler made of plain-woven light blue silk covering a stuffed sphere. Made by Ruth Wright of Exeter, Pa., who was registered in the Westtown Friends School, Oct. 1814. Couched blue silk longitudinal lines; tropics of Capricorn and Cancer done in red silk; equator, Arctic, and Antarctic circles in white silk; the continents and countries are outlined in white thread in a very fine couching stitch; names are in black ink. Diam. 16″ (40.64 cm); acc. no. 69.46.*

Figure 14

Figure 14. *Rare miniature, or sample, hand towel with pink and green flowers in satin, outline, and seed stitches. "Christina Hessin" and the date, "1815," embroidered in German script in outline stitch. Bands of fringe and drawn work all in white. Probably from Pennsylvania; H. 23½" (59.69 cm), W. 8¾" (22.22 cm); acc. no. 67.1266.*

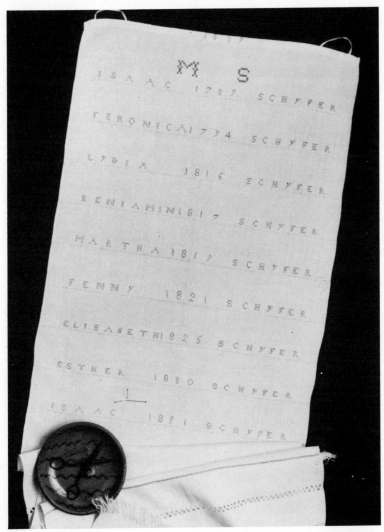

Figure 15

Figure 15. *Hand towel with a genealogical record of the Schyfer family worked in red cross stitch spaced with narrow bands of drawn work. The given names suggest that this was a Mennonite family in Pennsylvania. Dated 1839; H. 55⁹⁄₁₆″ (141.12 cm), W. 18⅛″ (46.05 cm); acc. no. 57.117.*

Figure 16

Figure 16. *Three stiffly posed, German-style flowers, in red and navy crewel yarns, are embroidered in outline stitch on a linen ground. Three smaller flower trees and "FROHICA BRAIDT" are worked in cross-stitched cotton yarns. Probably from Pennsylvania; 1820–40; H. 64½"*
(163.83 cm), W. 16⅝" (42.24 cm);
acc. no. 69.1146.

by embroidery into a regular design. Mrs. Mary Cary's advertisement in the *New York Mercury* of September 24, 1753, included "Dresden Work in all its variations."

Needle-made lace of the type found in samplers was used on baby caps and decorative handkerchiefs and aprons (Figure 11). Period newspaper advertisements show that one could also buy ready-made items decorated with Dresden work.

Beginning early in the nineteenth century, schools began to place more emphasis on teaching academic subjects to young women. In addition to the "essentials" of religion, needlework, art, and music, many schools started to offer science, literature, French, and geography. Map samplers were one result of this extended curriculum (Figure 12), although the making of conventional map samplers was far more common in England than in America. At Westtown, a Friends school near Philadelphia, the girls embroidered globes, a type not found elsewhere (Figure 13).

Hand towels made by the Pennsylvania Germans represent another sampler variant (Figures 14, 15, and 16). Many display names, alphabets, cross-stitched designs, drawn work; a few have genealogies. They bear dates ranging from the 1780s to the 1880s. These hand towels often had two small loops sewn to the top so that they could be hung on pegs or nails on the back of a door. These were the most practical of all the samplers because they were more than just demonstration pieces. However, so many have survived that it is doubtful they received much active service. Today, they are popularly known as show towels.

Canvas Work

What is called needlepoint today was commonly referred to as canvas work until the early nineteenth century. Occasionally, it was called tapestry work. True woven tapestries were very rare in America, but fine canvas work made excellent imitations of those elegant, exotic fabrics. We usually think of canvas as a coarse, heavy fabric, but the 1771 edition of *The Encyclopaedia Britannica* gives this definition: "a very clear unbleached cloth of hemp, or flax, wove very regularly in little squares. It is used for working tapestry with the needle, by passing the threads of gold, silver, silk, or wool through the intervals or squares."

Much finer canvas was available in the eighteenth century than today. The finest needlework canvas available today is woven twenty-four threads per inch. Eighteenth-century canvas ranged from eighteen to fifty-two threads per inch. When the lighting facilities of the period are taken into consideration, it is astounding to see canvas work of that fineness. Canvas was advertised frequently in colonial newspapers, and it was almost always listed under "imported" items. *The Boston Weekly News Letter* for June 7, 1750, carried this notice: "Imported in the last Ship from London, and to be Sold by Henrietta-Marie Caine, at the Sign of the Fan—broad and narrow yellow canvas."

Until the nineteenth century, the warp and weft yarns formed even, square holes in the canvas ground. With the advent of Berlin patterns, variations in the canvas weave emerged. In some, every tenth warp thread was of a contrasting color to facilitate counting squares. In others, the threads were woven in pairs so that both coarse and fine details could be worked on the same piece. Appearances are deceiving. Although these paired threads were not used until the mid-nineteenth century, worn areas of earlier pieces, particularly those worked in the Irish stitch, suggest that they had been worked on double-thread canvas. In reality, the stitches have simply pulled the canvas out of shape over time.

Many of the stitches used for canvas work tended to distort

Figure 17

Figure 17. *Original tent-stitch chair seat worked on canvas. Background of dark blue crewel yarns with flowers and leaves in golds, greens. roses, and white. Chair, numbered "VI," descended in the Bangs family of Newport, R.I.; second half of 18th century; H. 14½" (36.83 cm), W. 19⅛" (48.59 cm); acc. no. 59.832.*

Figure 18

Figure 18. *Tent-stitched Indian in red, blue, yellow, and light brown crewel yarns with accents of silk. Black background worked in cross stitch with initials "MR" and a fainter "S." 1725–75; H. 11¼" (28.57 cm), W. 9⁹/₁₆" (21.74 cm); acc. no. 53.173.12.*

the fabric, which is the reason that embroidery frames were commonly used for canvas work. Before commencing her project, the needlewoman would sew a linen tape around the edge of her canvas. Cords stitched between the tape and the frame held the fabric taut. When old canvas work is remounted today, one occasionally encounters stretched cord holes.

Crewels were the predominant type of embroidery yarn used for American canvas work of the eighteenth century. A few examples also contain metallic yarns or silks, but these were usually used only as accents in combination with crewels.

Because canvas work has always been one of the most elegant and expensive forms of embroidery, it is not surprising to find that instruction in its techniques was offered so frequently. The many references made to the teaching of the tent, Irish, and Queen's stitches must have implied, perhaps intentionally, that proper instruction was essential for satisfactory results.

Figure 19

Figure 19. *Small tent-stitched picture with a beige ground, blue and red flowers and berries, and a surprised bird with a red wing and topknot. The canvas was originally nailed to the backboard. Penciled in modern hand on the backboard is "Lidia Wright/Sandwich, Mass./D [?] family." 1725–75; H. 10¼" (26.03 cm), W. 8⁵⁄₁₆" (21.10 cm); acc. no. 61.1779.*

Figure 20

Figure 20. *Double pocketbook worked in tent stitch that has stretched the canvas badly out of shape. Beige ground with polychrome flowers, lined and edged with bright pink wool. Pattern guidelines of brownish black are visible with an electron microscope. 1740–90; H. (folded) 4¼" (10.79 cm), W. 7¾" (19.68 cm); acc. no. 66.1040.*
Figure 21. *Reverse side of tent-stitched chair seat showing complete disregard for neatness. (Front side on Plate III)*

Newspaper advertisements, North and South, mentioned canvas work designs and designers. Most canvases with designs already drawn on them were probably imported, but these precursors of today's needlework kits were expensive. Lessons in drawing were available for those who wished to create their own designs. John Thomas, who taught academic subjects in a boy's school, noted in the Charleston *South Carolina Gazette* of January 30—February 6, 1753, that "he will also undertake to teach about 6 young ladies, to draw and shade with Indian ink pencil, which may not only serve as an amusement to their genius, but in some respects become serviceable to them in needlework."

Examination by electron microscope of several canvas-work pieces in the Winterthur collection discloses outlines of designs drawn in black or brown ink on the underlying canvas. A pocketbook with a repeating flame design in Irish stitch has but one motif inked in the center. Apparently it was common practice to use the center as the starting point for a repeating design.

Figure 21

Figure 22

Figure 22. *Poorly worked fishing lady in tent stitch on canvas of 23 stitches to the inch. Crewel and silk yarns used except for the arms and face, which are rather crudely painted in oils. Boston area; 1745–55; H. 17″ (43.18 cm), W. 16⅛″ (40.97 cm); acc. no. 62.587.*

Plate I

Plate I. *A sampler in transition. The older style is present in the
horizontal bands of designs, but the newer vine border and verses are also
present. Exquisite needlework in Queen's, cross, satin, and outline
stitches. Variations of this style sampler, usually with an added alphabet,
remained popular in the Philadelphia area for almost fifty years. Some of
the verses are from* Epigrams on Progress, *by John Hawkins of Boston. The
piece is signed "17E4 Elizabeth Rush her Work done in th year of her age."
The 3 in the year is backward, and the year of her age is missing. This
Elizabeth was probably the great-aunt of Dr. Benjamin Rush, one of the
signers of the Declaration of Independence. H. 18¼" (46.35 cm), W. 13"
(33.02 cm); acc. no. 75.116.*

Plate II

Plate II. *Surely this sampler received high marks in needlework class. The First Baptist Church of Providence, R.I., is carefully wrought in tent stitch between Queen's-stitched pillars with a cross-stitched arch and a rice-stitched sky. The background is solidly worked in satin stitch. Perhaps the date above the pillars and the "Wrought" date at the bottom indicate that this project took Susan Smith 6½ months to complete. This bears all the design characteristics found in known examples from Polly Balch's School in Providence. H. and W. 16¾" (42.54 cm); acc. no. 58.2879.* Plate III. *Tent-stitched canvas work from a design source similar to that of Figure 25; floral border breaks interestingly into the narrow green frame. Colors were originally much more brilliant: bright maroon pinks have faded to gray blues. (See back view of this in Figure 21.) Four of these chair seats are known, two at Winterthur and two at the Boston Museum of Fine Arts. Boston; 1740–60; H. 19¾" (50.16 cm), W. 23⅜" (59.38 cm); acc. no. 60.1039.2.*

Plate III

Plate IV

Plate IV. *Sarah Warren must have received much praise for her graduation-type tent-stitched "fishing lady" picture. The three groups of figures all occur separately in other known pieces of "Boston" needlework. Sarah was 18 when she dated this piece, and lived at that time in Barnstable, Mass. Shown in its original walnut-veneered frame with a carved gilt inner and outer band. Dated 1748; H. (frame) 25⅜" (64.46 cm), W. (frame) 52⅜" (133.04 cm); acc. no. 62.69.*

Canvas work, although expensive, wears extremely well. Two chair seats (Figures 17 and 29) and an easy chair (Figure 30) still bear their original canvas-work coverings. Unfortunately, when our ancestors took inventory of their household furnishings they used the generic term *work'd chair bottoms* to describe such chairs instead of specifying whether they were canvas work or crewel embroidery. The fact that more canvas-worked chair seats survive suggests that canvas work was the intended reference.

During the seventeenth and eighteenth centuries, the most popular canvas-work stitches were called tent, cross, Irish, and Queen's. The tent, or *ten*, stitch has retained its original name. This simple stitch is worked diagonally from square to square of the canvas (Figure 19). However, this stitch must be worked with crewel or silk yarns on a very fine canvas to prevent gaps between stitches. The tent stitch is ideal for intricate floral designs or scenes, even though it is very time-consuming. In those days, it was common to work the tent stitch in horizontal rows wherever possible, which, unfortunately, tended to stretch the work diagonally (Figures 20 and 24). This sort of distortion also can result from improper blocking after the work is finished, or the stitches themselves can restretch the fabric with the passage of time. To prevent distortion in modern canvas work, the tent stitch is worked in diagonal rows.

Needlewomen of the seventeenth and eighteenth centuries evidently had a total disregard for neatness on the underside of their work. The fineness with which the surface of a piece was worked had no relation to the appearance of the reverse of the piece. Long strands of one color frequently crossed several inches, and knots were present in most work. A typical example is the back (Figure 21) of a canvas-work chair seat (Plate III). On some fine linen samplers, this sloppiness can be observed even from the surface (Figure 6). Apparently, neatness on the back of embroidery was a virtue not adopted until late in the nineteenth century.

Scenic views featuring human figures against a landscape make up a large portion of the surviving tent-stitch work made during the middle years of the eighteenth century. Most of these

Figure 23

Figure 23. *Woman in red dress with white apron spinning yarn—similar pose appears in Figure 24. The arched upper corners are original. Unidentified "LI" embroidered in left-hand margin. Boston area; 1745–55; H. 24" (60.95 cm), W. 21" (53.34 cm); acc. no. 56.62.* **Figure 24.** *Tent-stitched scene stretched so badly out of shape that sides have been filled in with paint. Tradition of having been made by a member of the Whipple family of Salem, Mass.; almost identical scene worked by a member of the Bourne family of Salem, owned by the Boston Museum of Fine Arts. Date "1748" over door of the house in upper left. Linen canvas of 24 holes to the inch worked in wool, silk, and metallic yarns with glass beads for eyes. Design drawn in with gray paint. Boston area; H. 20¾" (52.70 cm), W. 44" (111.76 cm); acc. no. 65.1609.*

scenic views are traceable to the Boston area, where they were probably produced as graduation pieces from a particular school. They were ambitious efforts, requiring as much as a year or more of work, and they display varying degrees of proficiency (Plate IV versus Figure 22). While size and overall composition may vary from picture to picture, individual elements are often identical, varying only in color and workmanship. The repetition of subject matter and details suggests a common source of design, not only for such themes as the "fishing lady" but also for individual figures like dogs, houses, and trees. Nancy Graves Cabot (*Antiques*, December, 1941, p. 367) suggested that a seventeenth-century French engraving was the probable source for the figure of a woman carrying a distaff (Figure 25 and Plate III). Future research may disclose still more print sources. The popularity of the fishing lady motif may be explained by the popularity of fishing as an eighteenth-century courting pastime.

These scenic tent-stitch pictures were prominently displayed in the home, as was the example described in *The Boston Gazette*, May 23, 1757, as "a Chimney Piece imitating Adam and Eve in Paradise, wro't with a Needle after the best Manner."

Figure 24

Figure 25

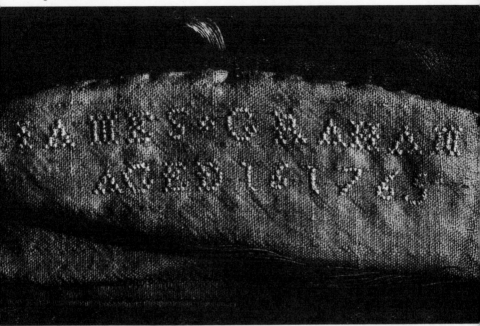

Figure 25. *Woman with basket of flowers on her head, worked by* "PRISCILLA A ALLEN DAUGHTER TO MR BENJAMIN ALLEN AND MRS ELISABETH ALLEN BOSTON JULY THE 20, 1746." *Source for this design was a 17th-century French engraving. Wool tent stitch on linen canvas of 22 holes to the inch; H. 21″ (53.34 cm), W. 15⅜″ (39.06 cm); acc. no. 62.588.* **Figure 26a.** *Irish-stitched pocketbook with cross-stitched name,* "JAMES GRAHAM AGED 16 1765," *on dark green lining under flap.* **Figure 26b.** *Outside: blue green ground with crown shapes in pinks, reds, and yellows. H. 5″ (12.70 cm), W. 8″ (20.32 cm); acc. no. 68.182.*

Figure 27

Figure 27. *Irish-stitched pocketbook in diamond-within-diamond design with a cross-stitched legend: "John Williamson 1775"; jagged lozenge shape outlined in black with gold, brown, rose, and blue; H. 4¾" (12.06 cm), W. 6⅝" (16.84 cm); acc. no. 58.2730.*

Figure 28

Figure 28. *Double Irish-stitched pocketbook in polychrome zigzag design. The name "Ephraim Pierce" is worked in single cross-stitched letters; 1740–90; H. (closed) 5⅛″ (14.30 cm), W. 9⅛″ (23.19 cm); acc. no. 61.1356.*

Figure 29

Figure 29. *Irish-stitched chair seat in carnation design of pinks and blues on a light brown background with ivory-color lozenge-shaped outlines. One of a set of N.Y. side chairs with seats worked by Elizabeth Banker before her marriage, in 1799, to General Samuel B. Webb. He was the private secretary to George Washington and founder of the Order of the Cincinnati. N.Y.; H. 16¼" (41.27 cm), W. 20⅜" (51.76 cm); acc. no. 59.2835.*

Another popular canvas-work stitch was the Irish stitch, which appears vertical on the surface but diagonal on the back. Each Irish stitch, as used in America, passed over three or four weft yarns; each tent stitch normally passed over only one warp yarn. Irish stitch, therefore, advanced the work more rapidly. Most pocketbooks (Figures 26, 27, 28, and Plate V) were worked in Irish stitch; other forms in which this stitch appears include chair seats (Figure 29), easy chairs (Figure 30), tablecloths (Figure 31), standing fire screens (Figure 32), hand fire screens (Figure 33), pincushions (Figure 34), and wall pockets (Figure 35).

The flamelike designs that were so often produced with Irish stitch probably gave rise to the twentieth-century term *flame stitch*. Actually, many other designs were worked with Irish stitch, including diamond-within-diamond patterns (Figure 27), zigzag patterns (Figure 28), carnations (Figure 29), and fanciful geometric shapes (Figure 26). Other names given to Irish stitch today are *Florentine*, *Bargello*, and *Hungarian*, but all these terms

Figure 30

Figure 30. *Irish-stitched upholstery for the front of an easy chair; carnation design in greens, brown, yellows, and rose on a cream-color ground. Blue green wool twill tape on edges. Sides and back of chair are dark green stamped wool; Philadelphia; 1740–50; H. (of chair) 46¼″ (117.47 cm), W. 34½″ (87.63 cm); acc. no. 58.557.*

Figure 31

Figure 31. *Irish-stitched tablecloth worked in a variety of patterns in shades of brilliant blues, greens, reds, and tan. Center area and lettering are done in rice stitch; two outer carnations are done in cross stitch. "MARY OOTHOUT/HER TABLE CLOA/TH SEPTEMBER/THE • 9 • 1759." Mary lived on Long Island and married into the Van Harlingen family of New Jersey; H. 29⅛" (73.99 cm), W. 51¾" (131.44 cm); acc. no. 66.74.*

Figure 32

Figure 32. Irish-stitched
fire screen with design
divided in jagged lozenge
shapes containing a variety
of centers. Dark green
background with beige,
yellow, browns, blue, and
rose pattern. Samplerlike
verse at bottom: "THIS WORK
IN HAND MY FRIENDS MAY HAVE
WHEN I AM DEAD AND LAID IN
GRAVE AND ALL MY BONES IS
ROTTEN THIS YOU SEE TO
REMEMBER ME THAT I AM NOT
FORGOTTEN TANNEKE PEARS HER
WORK DONE IN NEW YORK YEAR
1766." H. 22¾" (57.78
cm), W. 20" (50.80 cm);
acc. no. 65.2903. **Figure 33.**
Hand fire screen held to
protect the side of the
face nearest the fire.
Irish stitch with blue
green background, reds in
the center, and yellow on
the outer motifs all
outlined in black. 1725 – 75;
H. 18¾" (47.62 cm), W.
9¾" (24.76 cm); acc.
no. 57.120.

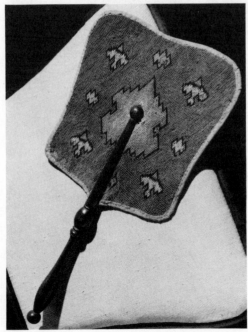

Figure 33

47

Figure 34

would have been meaningless to our ancestors—at least until the late nineteenth century.

Perhaps because the term is so descriptive, the cross stitch has mercifully retained its name through the ages. Cross stitch, frequently found in samplers for marking and embroidery accents, was also used in canvas work. On very fine canvas, the stitch sometimes crossed only one warp and weft yarn (Plate V), but it could also cross two yarns, which resulted in a coarser appearance (Figures 36, 37, and 38).

The Queen's stitch is one of the most difficult of the needlework stitches, a fact that undoubtedly accounts for its virtual extinction for the past century and a half. Even at the height of its popularity, from about 1780 to 1810, it was used only for very small items or for tiny accents (Figure 39 and Plate II). It was done by crossing several vertical stitches in the middle with a small horizontal stitch. Four or five of these stitches would surround a single interstice in the canvas to complete one unit. The regularly

Figure 35

Figure 34. *Irish-stitched pincushion in carnation design with shades of red, green, and brown. Initials "S" and "H" in lower corners; 1725—75; H. 4⅝" (11.76 cm), W. 3⅝" (9.22 cm); acc. no. 58.2236.* **Figure 35.** *Irish-stitched wall pocket in diamond-within-diamond design in shades of red, yellow, blue, and white. Embroidered in cross stitch is "17 M H 66." Heavy paper backing and lining; H. 10⅜" (26.36 cm), W. 8" (20.32 cm); acc. no. 58.1525.*

Figure 36

Figure 37

Figure 36. *Each cross stitch in this back panel for an easy chair covers two squares. The background is dark blue with polychrome flowers. Tradition of ownership in the Joshua Gardiner family of Boston, Mass.; 1725–75; H. 33¾" (85.72 cm), W. 23 ⅞" (60.65 cm); acc. no. 51.74.* **Figure 37.** *Cross-stitched pincushion with red, yellow, and blue floral design on a black background. "SI" and date "1776" are in red. H. 6¾" (17.14 cm), W.6" (15.24 cm); acc. no. 58.1581.*

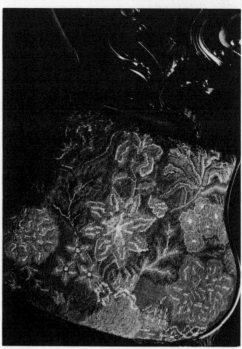

Figure 38. *Cross-stitched chair seat with polychrome floral pattern on a maroon background. 1725–75; H. 16½" (41.91 cm), W. 20½" (52.07 cm); acc. no. 60.1036.*

Figure 38

spaced holes created by so many stitches being worked into a common square produces an interesting texture that characterizes the Queen's stitch (Figures 40 and 42). Since silk was commonly used for this fine work, the Queen's-stitch pocketbook worked with crewel yarns is very unusual (Figure 41).

Early in the nineteenth century, a variation of canvas work, called Berlin work, emerged. About 1804, a printseller in Berlin devised a method of illustrating complete canvas-work designs on paper that was divided into a fine grid. Each square on the paper was intended to correspond to a square hole in the canvas. When the designs were hand-colored, as most of them were, it removed all need for creativity on the part of the embroiderer. Miss Lambert's *Ladies' Complete Guide to Needle-Work and Embroidery* (1859) defended Berlin work by saying, "the talented needlewoman, who even though she may have worked stitch for stitch

Plate V. *Group of three pocketbooks in different canvas-work stitches. Left: Extremely fine cross-stitched pocketbook bearing brown ink pattern guidelines for the design; 1740–80; H. 4" (10.16 cm), W. 7¼" (18.41 cm); acc. no. 61.1476. Center: A flamelike design worked in Irish stitch; 1740–90; H. 3⅞" (9.85 cm), W. 7⅛" (18.11 cm); acc. no. 58.2861. Right: Diamond design worked in silk Queen's stitch with heart-shaped silver clasp with bright-cut decoration and "м в" engraved initials. The name "Mary Remington" is worked in black cross stitch under the flap; she lived in East Greenwich or Warwick, R.I.; 1800–15; H. 4⁵⁄₁₆" (10.90 cm), W. 5³⁄₁₆" (13.20 cm); acc. no. 57.67.9.*

Plate V

Plate VI

Plate VI. *Irish-stitched book cover in a
flamelike design. One of the inscriptions
on the flyleaf reads: "John Gillingham His
Bible Bought [----]/Benjamin Franklin May^e
20^d 1740." Gillingham, a Philadelphia
cabinetmaker, labeled the table that the
Bible rests on, and the chair in the
background is attributed to him. 1740–60;
H. 15¾" (40.00 cm), W. 10½" (26.67
cm); acc. no. 61.102.1a,b.*

Plate VII

Plate VII. *Holder for a teakettle with two perky birds and marigoldlike flowers embroidered in crewel yarns on a fustian background. Worked in fine satin, bullion, chain, and French knot stitches. "HM 1773" in blue silk cross stitch. Identically shaped potholders, bearing similar designs, are found in the West Chester, Pa., area. H. 9½" (24.13 cm), W. 6¹⁵⁄₁₆" (17.62 cm); acc. no. 58.2540.*

Plate VIII

Figure 39

Plate VIII. *Delicate central urn with unusually spaced floral vines in an effective design always intended as a bedspread. Wear necessitated the addition of new linen to several worn areas. Stitches are finely executed in flat, chain, seed, cross, French knots, and back. 1720–70; H. 92″ (233.68 cm), W. 85½″ (225.90 cm); acc. no. 56.599.1.*
Figure 39. *Queen's-stitched double pocketbook with a flap. Dark green silk yarns for the background with rose, pink, and green strawberries in the centers of salmon-color diamonds. "Henry Row 1794" worked in cross stitch on a tent-stitched ground. H. (closed) 5″ (12.70 cm), W. 7⅛″ (18.11 cm); acc. no. 64.811.*

from the same pattern, produces what may be justly termed a 'painting with the needle.'"

Merino sheep, brought to the United States early in the nineteenth century, produced a yarn of very soft texture that was well adapted to Berlin work. Another name for the new merino yarns was *zephyr* yarns.

The Victorian preference for a bold, even strident, palette revealed itself frequently in Berlin work. By 1858, the introduction of synthetic aniline dyes helped to provide an even broader and more brilliant range of colors. Unfortunately, many of these colors have faded badly.

As Berlin work done with merino wools grew in popularity, more coarsely woven canvases were used. Rarely were they finer

Figure 40

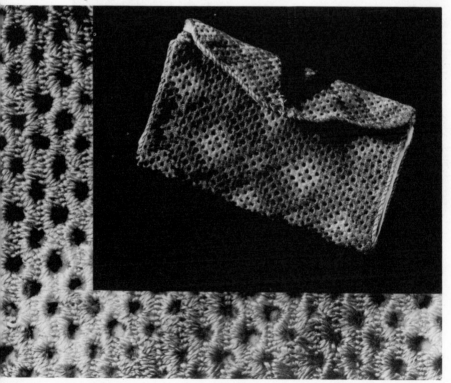

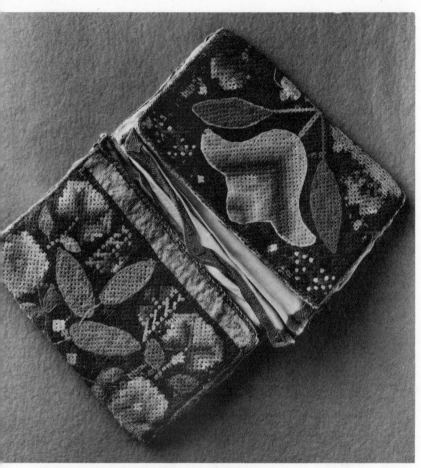

Figure 41

Figure 40. *Queen's stitch in silk yarns on canvas forming a small pocketbook. Green ground with shades of blue and salmon lined with striped silk. Written on lining, in 18th-century script, is "this Pocket Book worked by Mary Wright/1758." Mary lived in Middletown, Conn., and married Richard Alsop in 1760. (See Figures 87 and 88 for her knitted work.) H. 2¾" (6.98 cm), W. 4½" (11.43 cm); acc. no. 553.9.* **Figure 41.** *Unusual double pocketbook worked in Queen's stitch with crewel yarns. The name "THOMAS YARDLEY 1755" is worked in fine eyelet stitches. Colors are green, yellow, red, and blue on a medium brown ground. H. 5½" (13.98 cm), W. 7" (17.78 cm); gift of Mrs. Grace Erb; acc. no. 61.462.*

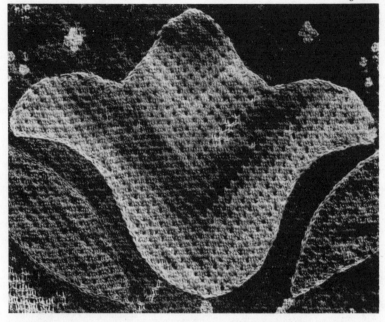

Figure 42

Figure 43

Figure 44

Figure 42. *Close-up of Figure 41 showing the crewel yarn in Queen's stitch with a tulip and leaves outlined in chain stitch.* **Figure 43.** *Irish-stitched bag in shades of brown, blue, and cream merino yarn. Horizontal stitches used to fill gaps resulting from this type of revival zigzag pattern. 1830–70; H. 6″ (15.24 cm), W. 6½″ (16.51 cm); acc. no. 5,9.749.* **Figure 44.** *Chair seat worked in merino yarns in Irish stitch on canvas with every tenth thread blue. Tan background with a revival design of carnations outlined in black with shades of purple, orange, brown, and green. Faded and badly worn with missing areas. 1825–70; H. 23⅛″ (58.75 cm), W. 23½″ (59.69 cm); acc. no. 69.1064.*

Figure 45

Figure 45. *Child's slippers worked in Irish stitch with blue, white, and tan merino yarns in a zigzag design. 1830–70; H. 5½″ (13.97 cm), W. 2″ (5.08 cm); acc. no. 60.133.*

than twenty yarns to the inch. New types of canvases were developed to facilitate the transfer of designs. Florence Hartley, in *The Ladies' Hand-Book of Fancy and Ornamental Work* (1859), described canvases woven with paired threads in warp and weft as "Penelope Canvas, so called from its having the appearance of canvas [in] which the work has been unpicked." This description probably refers to unpicking Irish stitch work on the older type canvases. Several mid-nineteenth-century authors used this same cumbersome description for Penelope canvas.

American women produced unbelievably large quantities of Berlin work. It decorated almost every imaginable article of clothing and home furnishing. From 1830 to 1870, it eclipsed practically all other types of needlework (Figures 43, 44, and 45). As Berlin work proliferated, designs degenerated into saccharine sentimentality. People tired of it, and, by the early 1880s, the author of *Art Needlework* observed that "The era of Berlin wool work has happily passed away."

Although its popularity waned, canvas work never completely died out, and now it is enjoying a renaissance. Today, as in the eighteenth century, the design is drawn directly on the canvas; the difference is that now commercially painted needlework canvases include the complete pattern in color.

Crewelwork Embroidery

Many people today think of *crewel* as a particular type of embroidery. At least since Shakespeare's time, however, crewel, in a variety of spellings, has referred to a yarn rather than a technique. Crewels are two-ply, slackly twisted, worsted yarns, and they are used for canvas work, as well as for the more openly designed embroidery commonly called crewelwork.

Inventories of household goods show the presence of crewel yarns in American homes from the middle of the seventeenth century. In 1687, Samuel Sewall, Boston merchant and magistrate, ordered from London "white Fustian" and "green worsted to work it" sufficient to make one complete set of bed hangings and the coverings for six chairs. His daughters, who were about to start school, were no doubt well occupied in crewel embroidery for some time following receipt of these materials.

The fustian requested by Sewall was a twill-woven fabric intended to serve as the fabric base for crewel embroidery (Plate VII). Usually it was woven of cotton and linen, but it could consist solely of cotton. Dimity was another material used for the same purpose (Figure 46). Resembling today's fine corduroy, it was also a blend of cotton and linen, although some all-cotton dimity grounds survive. The most popular background material for American crewel embroidery, however, was plain-woven linen.

Designs for crewel embroidery came from a variety of sources, including the embroiderer's own imagination. For less creative people, skilled relatives or friends, male and female alike, might create original designs. Needlework teachers, engravers, lesser artists, and tailors advertised their willingness to provide embroidery designs. It was said of a runaway mulatto servant woman, described in the *Providence Gazette* of July 30, 1763, that "she affects politeness, and is very ingenious at Drawing, Embroidery, and almost any kind of curious Needlework."

These designs were marked in ink on the fabric. Sometimes the designs also suggested the appropriate stitches to use. One un-

Figure 46

Figure 46. *Bed hanging, on
a cotton and linen dimity
background, embroidered in
polychrome crewels and silks.
A hunter with a stick, horn,
and three dogs chases a rabbit
on the moundlike hills near
a shepherd with his sheep.
The design is repeated
every 49 inches. Stitches
are long and short satin,
outline, and chain.
The exceptional fineness
(about 48 to 50 stitches
to the inch) and evenness
(rows are less than ⅛″
high) strongly suggest
professional embroidery.
Tradition of ownership in
William Penn's family;
however, the record of
descent is cloudy. The set
has been considerably
altered several times and
is in fragile condition.
Whether it was worked in
England or America is moot.
1680–1740; acc. no. 57.1285.*
Figure 47. *The inked design
is evident on this unfinished
band probably intended as a
petticoat border. On the
flower above the quizzical
cow, dots indicate seed
stitches or French knots.
Stitches are Roumanian
couching, outline, French
knots, seed, satin, and
darning. Brilliant polychrome
coloring. 1700–75; H. 7¼″
(18.41 cm), W. 95″
(241.30 cm); acc. no. 62.33.*

Figure 47

65

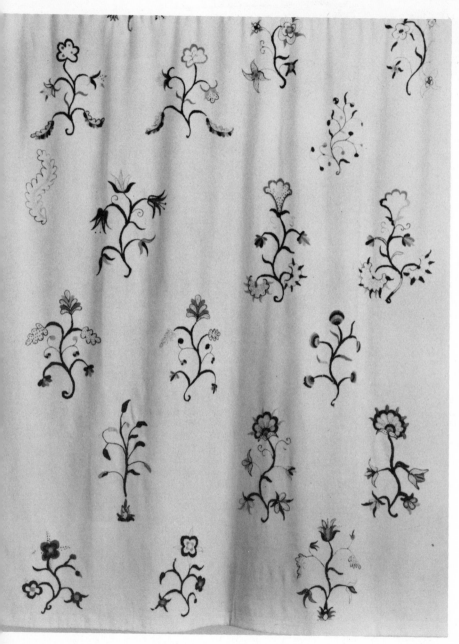

Figure 48

Figure 49

Figure 48. *Headcloth embroidered in four shades of
blue crewel yarn on plain-woven linen. Probably not
in its original form, as many sections have been
pieced together. 1750–1800; H. 62½″ (158.75 cm),
W. 61¼″ (155.47 cm); acc. no. 65.2507.* **Figure 49.**
*Bedspread with a strapwork design. Polychrome floral,
crewel embroidery worked over and around the tape. The
small tree at one end with a large cock perched on top
is thought to represent the Hancock family. John
Hancock probably inherited this spread from his uncle,
Thomas Hancock, who had adopted him. Thomas Hancock
had been apprenticed to Samuel Gerrick, whose wife Sarah
may have made this spread for Thomas Hancock when he
married in 1730. Many areas have been appliquéd onto
newer linen. The sides were possibly valances at one
time. Stitches are flat, outline, satin, buttonhole,
and seed. Boston; 1725–50; H. 112″ (284.48 cm), W.
78½″ (199.39 cm); acc. no. 52.358.1.*

67

finished piece (Figure 47) shows dots on the inked design, indicating the designer's intent for seed stitches or French knots to be used in these places.

The earliest major application of crewelwork was probably for large bed hangings to enclose the master bed. During the early colonial period, this bed was usually located in the parlor and was therefore seen by all visitors. Draping this very important piece of furniture with elegant fabric was one way of indicating status and wealth in the stratified society of, for example, Puritan New England. Printed fabrics were still rare, and silk brocades and damasks were too expensive for all but the very wealthy. Linen cloth and woolen yarn were available as domestic or imported products and were relatively cheaper. The varied design possibilities afforded by colorful crewels made them extremely appealing for the challenging and expensive task of ornamenting the master bed. Few complete sets of crewel bed hangings survive. A

Figure 50

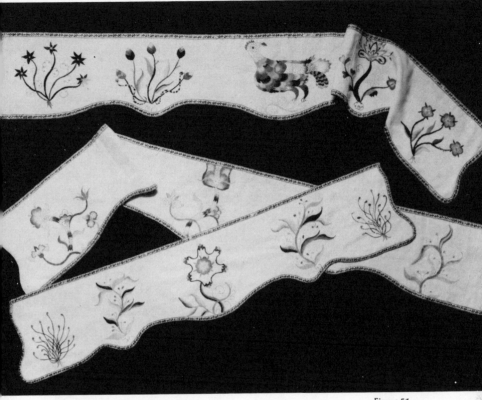

Figure 51

Figure 50. *Bedspread with two shades of blue crewels worked in outline, satin, and flat stitches on a coarse, cotton twill ground. Four-inch raveled fringe on three sides. Said to have been owned in the Hasbrouch family of Newburgh, N.Y. 1750–1800; H. 104″ (264.16 cm), W. 80″ (203.20 cm); acc. no. 67.65.*
Figure 51. *Valances of multicolored crewels with fanciful flower sprays and a saucy bird. Blue and white printed tape around edges; however, piecing of the valances and the addition of a lining suggest that they are not in their original form. The parrotlike bird and seaweed flower sprays are related to a number of Connecticut crewel embroideries. Stitches are flat, bullion, buttonhole, seed, and outline. 1740–80; H. (short one) 11¼″ (28.57 cm), W. 56″ (142.24 cm); H. (longer ones) 11¼″ (28.57 cm), W. 79½″ (201.93 cm); acc. no. 54.14.4–.6.*

Figure 52

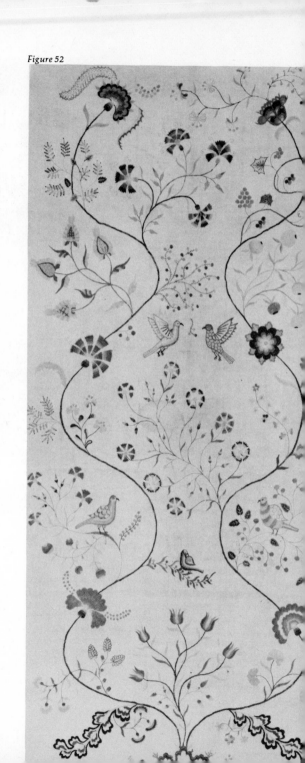

Figure 53

Figure 52. *Polychrome side panel with five birds inhabiting a remarkable vine containing sprays of carnations, grapes, lemons, bachelor's buttons, and tulips. Stitches are flat, outline, back, satin, buttonhole, bullion, weaving, and ladder. A pair of very similar design is owned by the Shelburne Museum. Probably from Massachusetts; 1750–1800; H. 70½″ (179.07 cm), W. 33″ (83.82 cm); acc. no. 57.44.1a.*

Figure 53. *Back of a child's dress with polychrome crewel flower sprigs. Stitches are flat, outline, trellis couching, and buttonhole. Dress probably made from a used bed curtain and the sleeve ruffles from another piece. Connecticut; 1730–80; L. (shoulder to hem) 24¾″ (62.86 cm); gift of Mrs. Alfred C. Harrison, Mrs. Reginald P. Rose, Mrs. Rodney M. Layton, and Mrs. Lammot du Pont Copeland; acc. no. 67.255.*

71

full set would include headcloth (Figure 48), bedspread (Figures 49 and 50), three or four valances (Plate X and Figure 51), and six side curtains (Figure 52).

Strangely, the author found only one possible reference to crewel window curtains, and no surviving examples are known. References to window hangings of any sort are rare in early colonial records. When they do appear, they are usually listed *en suite* with bed hangings.

Crewel embroidery also decorated clothing and accessories, such as dresses (Figure 53), petticoat borders (Figures 47 and 54), pockets (Figure 55), and pocketbooks (Figures 56 and 57). Other forms on which crewel embroidery appears include chair seats (Figure 58), usually worked solidly, potholders (Plate VII), and pictures (Figures 59 and 60).

Figure 54

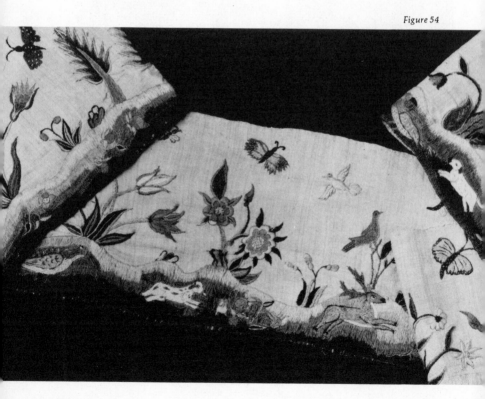

Plate IX

Figure 54. *Polychrome petticoat border with a white spotted dog watched by a curlew as a deer romps on the hillocks. All sense of proportion is forgotten on this naive band that may have been a preliminary piece done by a girl in school before she progressed to a more formal canvas-work "chimney piece." Several similar bands are owned by the Boston Museum of Fine Arts. Stitches are flat, outline, fishbone, satin, and bullion. Boston area; 1740–60; H. 8" (20.32 cm), W. 96" (219.07 cm); acc. no. 57.52.3.* **Plate IX.** *With but three shades of blue, the central design on this bedspread vigorously radiates motion. Stitches are Roumanian couching, darning, outline, cross, seed, and satin. Probably from Connecticut; 1740–80; H. 101" (256.54 cm), W. 66" (167.64 cm); acc. no. 65.2504.*

74

Plate X

Plate XI

Plate X. *Valances and headcloth in unusual grayed tones of blues, wine reds, and puce which were perhaps specially dyed or selected by the embroiderer. Most of the design elements are very solidly filled with Roumanian couching, outline, bullion, French knots, and weaving stitches. 1730—80. Valances: H. (of longest) 11¹³⁄₁₆″ (29.99 cm), W. 73³⁄₁₆″ (185.90 cm); acc. no. 55.749.5-.7. Headcloth: H. 62½″ (159.75 cm), W. 56¾″ (144.14 cm); acc. no. 55.749.2.* **Plate XI.** *Needlework picture featuring a single tree, similar in design to those found in Indian palampores, and rabbits bouncing on small hillocks. Very fine silk and metallic thread embroidery on a buff silk moiré taffeta ground. Stitches are satin, French knots, seed, couching, and outline. One flower has a center raised with padding and couched in metallic yarns. Purchased with another picture with the same ground and similar embroidery, signed ''Mary King 1754.'' She probably attended the same school as Sally Wistar (Figure 66). Pennsylvania; 1750—69; H. 16″ (40.64 cm), W. 17⅜″ (44.14 cm); acc. no. 66.977.*

Plate XII

Figure 55

Plate XII. *The weeping willow and cedar trees are elements frequently found in mourning pictures of this period, but this embroideress was too exuberant to include somber colors and a tomb. Cream-color silk satin ground with silk and chenille embroidery in satin, outline, French knots, and fern stitches. Attributed to Ann Jefferis Wilson of Philadelphia, Pa., and Odessa, Del.; 1800–20; H. 25¹⁵/₁₆″ (65.88 cm), W. 18³/₁₆″ (46.20 cm); Odessa Properties, Winterthur Museum; acc. no. 71.1248.* **Figure 55.** *Pocket made to be tied around the waist to hold miscellaneous items. Plain-woven linen ground with Roumanian couching, outline, chain, and ladder stitches in three shades of blue, with touches of gold and beige. 1730–80; H. 16″ (41.27 cm), W. 13″ (33.02 cm); acc. no. 58.2051.*

Figure 56

Figure 56. *Solidly worked pocketbook with inked design lines on the background (seen with an electron microscope). Blue green ground with flowers in tans, rose, and blue. The flat stitch was used for the ground and flowers, outline stitch for the edges; small bits of satin stitch are used as accents in the semicircular flower. 1740–90; H. 4½" (11.43 cm), W. 7¹/₁₆" (17.93 cm); acc. no. 66.744.* **Figure 57.** *A pocketbook solidly worked with red crewels in flat stitch with the design edged in outline stitch. Vivid shades of green, blue, red, and brown. 1740–90; H. (closed) 3½" (8.89 cm), W. 6½" (16.51 cm); acc. no. 62.110.*

Bed hangings—known then as bed furniture—changed toward the end of the eighteenth century. The earlier functional practice of enclosing the bed completely gave way to merely decorating it with hangings. Emphasis was on the coverlet and the valances, the latter often taking the form of decorative swags.

During the same period and into the first quarter of the nineteenth century, crewel-embroidered blankets were popular (Figure 61). They not only made attractive bed covers but provided warmth as well. The coarse background of the blanket required heavier denier crewel yarns than did linen backgrounds. Some blankets had colorfully woven squares that enclosed the crewel designs (Figure 62).

Figure 57

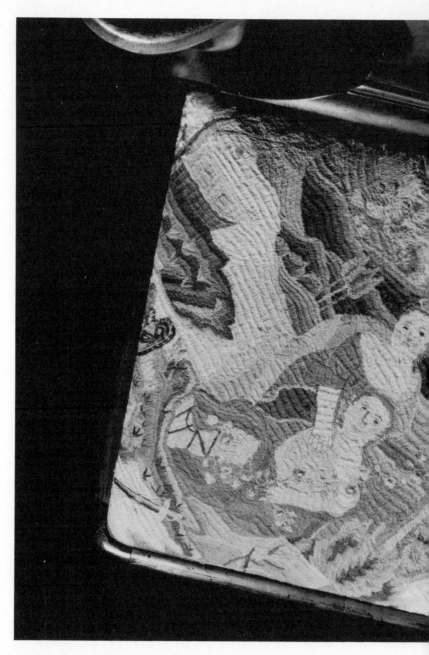

Figure 58

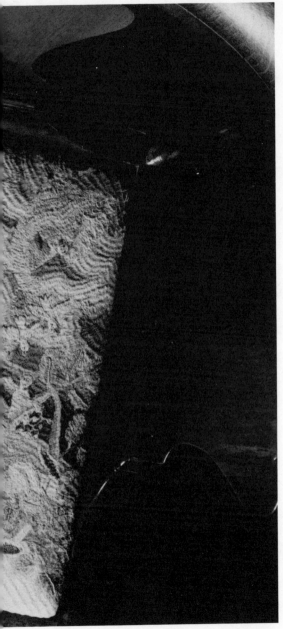

Figure 58. *Solidly worked multicolored needlework adapted for a corner chair. Stitches are Roumanian couching, outline, bullion, and French knots. Crudely drawn woman and man (the latter in sandals and a toga with a sword at his feet), rowboat docked in the left corner, and six other small figures flying blithely around the sky and landscape. 1730–80; H. 15½" (39.37 cm), W. 15½" (39.37 cm); acc. no. 61.1190.*

Figure 59. *Brilliantly colored crewelwork picture, solidly worked but very crudely drawn. Probably done by a novice or very young girl. (Closely related in feeling to petticoat border in Figure 54.) Boston area; 1740–60; H. 9" (27.86 cm), W. 15" (38.10 cm); acc. no. 58.2231.*

Figure 59

Crewelwork, together with most embroidery traditions in America, owes a great debt to its English heritage. Early American crewel is difficult to distinguish from contemporaneous English examples, for American needlework often used English background fabrics, English designs, and English crewels. As time went on, however, certain practices arose that help to distinguish American work from English work. American work, for example, has a more limited vocabulary of stitches on a given piece than English work—many large examples of American crewelwork disclose only three to five different stitches. In general, American designs are usually smaller and less complicated than their English

counterparts, and, frequently, more of the background fabric is visible.

The stitches on American work also tend to be less complicated than those used in England. Roumanian couching and flat stitch (very similar in appearance and technique) are usually indicative of American work (Figure 65). (Unfortunately, we seem to have lost the eighteenth-century names for both of these stitches, which today are known by many different names.) Some authorities attribute the popularity of these stitches to the fact that neither required as much yarn as the satin stitch—an important consideration during a time when imported crewels were rather

Figure 60

Figure 60. *Whimsical birds with oversize feet worked by Elizabeth Taylor of Chester County, Pa., in 1785. This is the crudest and perhaps earliest of the three pieces known to have been worked by her. The original color scheme was almost gaudy: what are now soft browns, rose, and green were once vivid maroons, purples, dark brown, and green. Stitches are outline, satin, and bullion. The date "1785" is in black silk cross stitch and the initials are in green silk cross and eyelet stitches. The drawing was done in brown ink. H. 11⅛″ (28.27 cm), W. 8⅞″ (22.55 cm); acc. no. 58.2762.* **Figure 61.** *Cream wool ground with a vine border design worked in three shades of blue crewel yarns. Blue wool twill tape trims the edge. Stitches are Roumanian couching, outline, and cross, with numerous mended areas. Thought to be either a crib blanket or a tea cloth; history of ownership in New Hampshire; 1750–90; H. 28⅝″ (72.72 cm), W. 41⅝″ (105.74 cm); acc. no. 64.20.*

Figure 61

Figure 62. *Blanket with twill-woven cream ground and woven rose-color squares. Crewel-embroidered flower forms, in blues, cream, and rose grace each square. A stencil or pattern must have been used because the design outlines are exactly repeated (the colors and stitches vary). Stitches are chain, outline, French knots, satin, and flat. The blanket is seamed down the center and has an applied rose-color fringe on three sides. 1780–1830; H. 75½″ (191.77 cm), W. 84″ (213.99 cm); acc. no. 69.1699.*

Figure 62

85

Figure 63

Figure 63. *Probably originally a side panel. The staring cow is smaller than the pineapple popping from the ground. Two graceful trees, resembling spring larch trees, add dignity to an otherwise humorous design. The rolling hills in the foreground probably were once solidly worked rows of flat stitch. These have been lost and replaced by appliquéd linen. The trees resemble those on several pieces in the Boston Museum of Fine Arts and one privately owned example, so perhaps all are from the same source. Massachusetts; 1700 – 50; H. 113″ (287.02 cm), W. 35″ (88.90 cm); acc. no. 65.2513.2a.* **Figure 64.** *Unfinished, brilliantly colored panel, perhaps intended as a valance, portraying a harvest scene. The birds gaily compete with the people for the ripe cherries, while the animals play on the hills. Silk yarn has been used for some accents. Stitches are predominantly Roumanian couching with outline, seed, French knots, and satin. This work is attributed to Mary Dodge Burnham of Newburyport, Mass.; 1725 – 50; H. 16¼″ (41.27 cm); W. 61⅞″ (157.17 cm); acc. no. 62.12.*

Figure 64

Figure 65

Figure 65. *Squirrels romp on hills and chase a silk butterfly in a close-up of Figure 64 showing the use of Roumanian couching.*

expensive—but the amount of yarn saved would actually have been minuscule. Perhaps more realistic explanations of their popularity are the facts that both Roumanian couching and flat stitch were easily mastered and were more readily controlled over relatively large, solid areas than satin stitch.

With the beginning of direct American trade with China following the Revolutionary War, silk yarns and fabrics from that country became more available and less expensive than they had been before the war, when the colonists had had to deal with British middlemen. The shimmering luster of these yarns and fabrics speeded the desire in America to replace the less exotic crewel embroidery. Interior design in the Federal period favored lightly styled furniture with delicate inlays, veneers, and glistening fabrics. In this new context, crewelwork seemed old-fashioned, and it was gradually packed away.

Silk Work

Except for work in metallic yarns of gold or silver, silk embroidery has always been considered the most elegant type of needlework. Embroidered silks were sometimes highlighted with the precious metal threads.

Silk thread and cloth were expensive compared to other fibers. Attempts to raise silk worms were made throughout the colonial period in America, starting in Virginia as early as the mid-seventeenth century. Domestic silk production remained meager, in spite of occasional newspaper advertisements, such as this one published in *The Pennsylvania Gazette*, September 6, 1770: "All Persons, who have COCOONS, which they are desirous of having wound, are requested to bring them to the FILATURE, in this City." Imported silk thread "in shades" was readily obtainable in all the larger cities, but it was undoubtedly far more costly than crewel yarn or linen thread.

Most silk yarns were used on silk grounds, although silk yarns can also be found on grounds of other fibers. Fine silk yarns were particularly favored for needlework pictures. Pictures worked on silk grounds that date from the middle years of the eighteenth century are of finer-quality embroidery than those stitched later. The Philadelphia area produced a particularly exquisite group of these pictures (Figure 66 and Plate XI).

A smaller group of interesting pictures, worked on black silk grounds with much coarser stitches than the Philadelphia group, were done in the Boston area. The picture of the strolling couple (Figure 67) was possibly done in Salem, Massachusetts. Their costumes date this piece in the 1760s or 1770s. Parasols were probably included in the design because they were a recent novelty.

Few examples of silk embroidery known to have been done in the southern colonies survive. Southern women in urban centers at least had the opportunity to learn if they responded to advertisements such as Martha Logan's in the *South Carolina Gazette* (Charleston), August 1–8, 1754, in which she stressed instruction in "Embroidery with Silk, Cruels, or Silver and Gold Thread."

Figure 66

Figure 67

Figure 66. *A precariously perched bird stares at the world from a finely worked flowering tree. White moiré silk taffeta background with bright polychrome silk embroidery in satin, French knots, and outline stitches. In script on the original backboard is "The gift of Sarah Wistar to her great Neice Catharine Wistar/1789/Worked in the year. 1752." This is one of a pair of pictures Sarah did when she was 14 years old. She was the daughter of Caspar Wistar, a manufacturer of glass in Salem County, N.J. However, the family lived in Philadelphia. A narrow linen tape, sewn around all the edges, held the work on the embroidery frame. A piece of wool flannel was originally laid under the embroidery, padding it from the wooden backboard. Pa.; H. 9½″ (24.13 cm), W. 7″ (17.78 cm); acc. no. 64.120.2.* **Figure 67.** *A pastoral scene with two women parading their finery, including a parasol, while one man smokes a pipe and another picks berries. Black silk background with outline, seed, and extremely long satin stitches. Shades of green, turquoise, brown, and white portray hills, deer, dogs, and strawberries similar to those associated with the Boston-Salem area. 1760–70; H. 15½″ (39.37 cm); W. 22¼″ (56.51 cm); gift of Mrs. Alfred C. Harrison, Mrs. Reginald P. Rose, Mrs. Rodney M. Layton, and Mrs. Lammot du Pont Copeland; acc. no. 59.1883.*

Toward the end of the eighteenth century, scenic views and still lifes became increasingly popular. Many of these designs were professionally drawn on the silk. Others were drawn by the young ladies themselves as they applied newly acquired skills learned in one of the numerous art classes so fashionable at the time. Some girls simply traced their designs from popular prints of the day. A few needleworkers ambitiously imitated the appearances of engraving in designs called "print-works" (Figure 68). By 1800, many silk pictures were embellished with watercolors.

After the Revolutionary War, American ships began direct trade with China. As a consequence, silk yarns and fabrics became less expensive. Silk embroidered pictures became even more popular, and their sparkling, delicate appearance blended well with the satinwood inlays and slim lines that characterized Federal furniture.

Figure 68

M. TEN. EYCK. 1805.

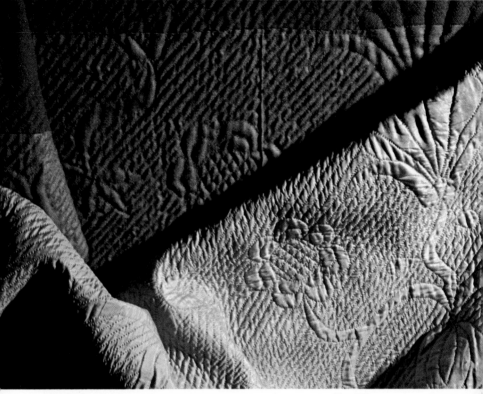

Plate XIII

Figure 68. *Mourning picture, styled to look like an engraving, worked in black fibers that are probably human hair. The face, clouds, and little dog are shaded with paint. No Gothic church like the one shown had been built in the United States at the time this was made. Written on the tomb at left is "In Memory of Henry Ten Eyck obit 1st July 1794 Æ 8 Yrs. & 5 Mths," and on the tomb at right "In Memory of Catharine Ten Eyck Obit: 25th Augt 1797 Æ : 18 Months." On the black and gold border is, "M • TEN • EYCK • 1805." Margaret Bleeker Ten Eyck, who worked this, was married to Harmanus Ten Eyck, who was the great-great-grandfather of Henry Francis du Pont. Albany, N.Y.; H. 22¼" (56.48 cm), W. 15¼" (38.73 cm); acc. no. 58.2877.* **Plate XIII.** *Originally a petticoat of light green plain-woven silk with dark blue wool lining and interlining of blue wool. A one-piece quilt, quilted in very fine running stitches. 1750 – 1800; H. 36⁵⁄₁₆" (92.22 cm), L. 117¾" (299.08 cm); acc. no. 69.1110.*

Plate XIVa. *A true friendship or bride's quilt with the name of the donor on each square. The border is pieced, but the 20 designs are appliquéd. A few flowers are three-dimensional with the petals attached only at their centers. Inked details and chain-stitch embroidery enhance some squares. It is possible that some of these squares were purchased from a professional quilter. Baltimore, Md.; H. 122⅝″ (311.48 cm), W. 106½″ (270.51 cm); acc. no. 69.571.* **Plate XIVb.** *Detail of one square. Dated 1854.* **Plate XV.** *The tall vase of flowers shown here is known to have been block-printed by John Hewson of Philadelphia. Because this same vase appears in several quilts surrounded by entirely different elements, it is probably an example of a "patch" sold just to decorate an appliquéd quilt. The outer flowers are from English print factories. 1780–1800; L. 86½″ (219.71 cm), W. 83″ (210.82 cm); acc. no. 64.1001.*

Plate XIVb

Plate XV

Plate XVI

Plate XVI. *A vigorous, balanced design,
but not identical on each side. Heavy,
wool yarn stitched in a raised-loop
running stitch. Initials "NC" and date
"1819" in a scalloped medallion at the
top. New England; H. 93" (236.22 cm)
W. 97" (246.38 cm); acc. no. 64.1641.*

Figure 69

Figure 69. *Landscape displaying total disregard for perspective. The river, sky, and many details are painted in watercolors. The foliage on the trees and shrubs is worked in hundreds of French knots in shades of blue, green, white, and brown. Satin stitch for the ground and some of the flowers. 1790–1815; H. 18½″ (46.99 cm), W. 22⅜″ (56.84 cm); acc. no. 67.528.*

Flowers and birds have always been favorite needlework themes, and some enthusiastic compositions show almost an over-abundance of both (Plate XII). Statements of pride in local buildings, homes, and cities account for another group of subjects (Figure 69). Patriotic themes abounded (Figures 70 and 71). The design of Figure 71 derives from an engraving originally published in 1796 by Edward Savage. Probably his oil painting of the subject preceded this print, but it has been lost. It was called "Liberty. In the form of the Goddess of Youth: giving Support to the Bald Eagle." The print inspired many copies in oils, in watercolors, on velvet, in wax, and even reverse paintings on glass done by Chinese artists. The multiple symbolism of Liberty feeding an eagle, the key to the Bastille, an English Garter underfoot, and a Liberty cap above was immediately significant to contemporaries. This example demonstrates the attractive use of "spangles," the

Figure 70

Figure 70. *Revolutionary War scene based on a print—said to be one of the first representations of the American flag—titled "Lady Harriet Ackland," published in London, Nov. 15, 1784, by R. Pollard. Lady Ackland is attempting to visit her husband—wounded at the battle of Saratoga—with his valet, a female servant, and a minister. Plain and chenille yarns worked on a polychrome silk ground with faces, hands, river, sky, and other details painted. Mounted in its original gilt frame. 1785–1810; H. (of embroidery) 16⅞″ (42.87 cm), W. 20″ (50.80 cm); acc. no. 64.774.2.*
Figure 71. *The lady's face has a faintly oriental look, possibly because she was copied from a Chinese version of Edward Savage's painting and engraving titled, "Liberty. In the form of the Goddess of Youth; giving Support to the Bald Eagle." The foreground is worked in shaded chenille yarns; the dress is worked in silk yarns with very fine satin stitches and evenly spaced spangles. The quality of the painting done for the sky, eagle, and face does not approach the high standard of the embroidery. 1796–1820; H. 22⁷⁄₁₆″ (56.99 cm); W. 18¾″ (47.62 cm); acc. no. 69.1790.*

IN MEMORY of WA

Figure 72

Figure 72. *Memorial picture to George Washington on a cream cotton and silk twill ground. Superbly painted faces, sky, and house with silk chenille yarns for the trees and part of the urn; woolen yarns for part of the ground; and silk yarns for clothing and the remainder of the urn and ground; all in satin stitch. Design based on Samuel Seymour's engraving, "In Memory of General Washington and his Lady," published by J. Savage in Philadelphia in 1804 and 1814, and as a colored lithograph in 1840. Winterthur owns a mirror with a reverse painting on glass of this scene as well as a drawing of the scene done by a schoolboy in an art class. Black-painted border with gilt letters "IN MEMORY of WASHINGTON, Elizabeth Lane, Fecit, 1817." H. 14" (35.56 cm), W. 17" (43.18 cm); acc. no. 57.784.*

101

Figure 73

Figure 73. *Circular mourning picture
commemorating the death of Webster
Downing, who lived in Downingtown, Pa.
Penciled on the stretcher is "*MSD 1819,*"
for Mary Downing, who embroidered the
ground in chenille yarns, with silk
yarns in the satin stitch for trees,
clothes, and remaining hills.
Well-painted faces, arms, feet, and
clouds, all on a silk ground. Diam.
19¾" (50.16 cm); acc. no. 69.217.*

eighteenth-century term for sequins. It also contains chenille yarns, which were particularly favored for embroidered silk pictures. (In French, *chenille* means "caterpillar"—a most apt description.) The urn, raised and molded by padding underneath, was worked in silver threads.

Mourning pictures represent another popular theme in silk work. Collectors avoided them for years, probably, as Huckleberry Finn put it, because "they always give me the fantods." Recently, they have experienced a resurgence in popularity. When the revered George Washington died in 1799, a wave of popular mourning swept the country (Figure 72). Mourning became fashionable (Figure 73). Perhaps working a picture of the beloved's tomb was a good grief therapy. The standard vocabulary of mourning pictures consisted of tombs, weeping willows, angels, and downcast mourners. Female mourners are resplendent in diaphanous Empire gowns that imitated those of classical antiquity. This neoclassical affectation was found in all American decorative arts during the early nineteenth century.

Like canvas work, most silk embroidery was worked on an embroidery frame. Occasionally, the silk ground was backed with cotton or linen and the embroidery stitched through both layers. Examples reinforced in this manner have survived in better condition than those without the backing. A method of reinforcing silk pictures to be framed was to lace them directly to the backboard of the frame in which they were to be displayed. The silk picture made by Sarah Wistar (Figure 66) was found mounted in this manner—it had been laced through a series of holes drilled around the perimeter of the backboard about one-quarter inch in from the edge of the picture.

Quilts

Quilting represents both essential and fancy needlework. Quilts were utilitarian, but they also provided a vehicle for displaying decorative needlework prowess. Early wills and probate records listed them. The 1705 probate record for John Weir, a merchant of Charleston and Philadelphia, lists one in his great parlor that, judging from its description, must have been elegant: "A wrought Quilt lined in a Silk, valued at six pounds." Unfortunately, very few if any of the early quilts have survived. Examples dated earlier than 1750 are extremely rare.

In a time that found the heating of homes and public buildings grossly deficient, people took advantage of the insulative warmth inherent in quilts and adapted the technique for making clothing, including bonnets, vests, coats, and petticoats. In fact, some of the loveliest quilting ever done survives as petticoats. At one time, fashion dictated that the front panel of a skirt be open. Thus, petticoats were meant to be seen, and, by varying her petticoat, a woman could build a flexible wardrobe around a single stylish dress.

Having to sort out the wide variety of quilting techniques in use can be quite a confusing task. Basic to all methods, however, are three components; top layer; filler; and lining, or bottom layer. The bottom layer was usually cotton, but the filler might have been nearly anything—an old blanket, combed wool, or cotton wadding. Cotton batting for use as quilting filler was advertised in the *Essex Gazette* (Salem, Massachusetts) of May 11—18, 1773, as "cotton-wool." The composition of the top layer also varied; although it was frequently made of cotton—as are most quilts today—silk, wool, and linsey-woolsey tops were also used. Tops were of three general types, used either singly or in combination: one-piece, pieced, and appliquéd. There were also variations within these major categories.

Figure 74

Figure 75

Figure 74. *One-piece quilt with a dark green wool top and a tan wool lining. Quilted in a common feather design and diagonal lines in running stitch. 1775–1800; H. 99″ (251.46 cm), W. 96″ (243.84 cm); acc. no. 60.1129.* **Figure 75.** *Detail of the signature along one edge. Probably says "Abigail Godwin."*

Quilts described as having one-piece tops represent the simplest and probably the earliest type of quilt made in the colonies, even though the phrase "one-piece top" is inaccurate. The looms of the day, particularly domestic looms, produced fabrics that were, by today's standards, relatively narrow. Accordingly, the needlewoman would sew together several lengths of fabric, selvage to selvage, to obtain the necessary width for her quilt top. Stitching was then used to bind together the three quilt layers and to prevent the shifting of the filler (Figures 74 and 75). This stitching was done in patterns to create designs, and it is here that the artistry of the needleworker came into play. Because the overall effect of the quilt was entirely dependent upon the quality of the design and the execution of the stitches, it is understandable that some of the finest surviving quilts belong to this "one-piece top" category (Plate XIII). One-piece tops were usually a solid color, but printed fabrics were sometimes used (Figure 76).

Figure 76

Figure 77

Figure 76. *The face of this one-piece quilt is cream linen; the back has been block printed with the stamps found in this box of printing tools. The exterior of the box is covered with a Boston newspaper dated May 9, 1812. The box has descended in the Copeland-Waterman family of Hanover, Mass. The quilting is in a simple diamond design, and uses the running stitch. H. 89″ (226.06 cm), W. 87½″ (223.25 cm); acc. no. 69.575.*
Figure 77. *Blue and white pieced quilt with thirty-six 9″ squares in the center. Alternating squares are pieced with curved edges to an indigo discharge print. Fine, almost puckered, quilting in the background. Family history attributes this to Millicent Stevens Burdick; probably Watertown, N.Y.; 1820—54. H. 88″ (223.52 cm), W. 90″ (228.60 cm); gift of Frank A. McDermott; acc. no. 66.133.*

Figure 78

Figure 78. This early pieced quilt is virtually a compendium of the fabrics available in the U.S. around 1800. Probably, it has survived because it contains so many elegant fabrics. There are silks with Chinese hand embroidery, Chinese hand-painted silks, and a variety of damasks, brocades, yarn-dyed patterns, wools, and cottons. (See Figure 81 for details of newspapers found under the fabrics.) Attributed to Martha Agry Vaughn of Hallowell, Me.; 1800–20; H. 100" (254.00 cm), W. 104" (264.16 cm); acc. no. 57.48.

Figure 79

Figure 79. *Detail of an appliquéd quilt showing a block-printed design with the edges turned under and finely whipped down. The printed fabrics in this quilt were all made in England between 1815 and 1845. Thought to have been made by Eliza Ely Bready who lived in Philadelphia. H. 140" (355.60 cm), W. 139" (353.06 cm); gift of Marguerite L. Riegel; acc. no. 63.86.* **Figure 80.** *Quilt pieced with silks in muted shades of green, pink, blue, and beige. The center has a stuffed-work basket of fruit. Made by Rachel Goodwin Woodnutt (b. Nov. 25, 1787; d. Nov. 4, 1828) of Salem, N.J. H. 106" (269.24 cm), W. 113½" (288.29 cm); gift of Elizabeth Newlin Baker; acc. no. 60.34.3.*

In pieced quilts, the second major category, geometrically cut swatches of fabric were seamed together along their abutting sides in such a way that their raw edges faced the filler layer. Since only an expert needleworker could successfully piece designs with curved edges, straight-edged shapes were usually used (Figure 77). Pieced quilts were eminently practical; the seamstress could use scraps and remnants to create ingenious patterns, an early example of recycling (Figure 78). Probably more pieced quilts were produced than any other kind, but because they also received the hardest wear, few early examples have survived.

The third major form of quilting is called appliqué quilting. Textiles that were printed with fairly large designs were particularly amenable to this technique. The seamstress would cut out the

Figure 80

designs, leaving a narrow border around each one. These borders were turned under and pressed in place. Blind or decorative stitches were then used to sew the pieces to a background fabric (Figure 79). Sometimes the edges were left raw, and rows of chain or feather stitching, which prevented the fabric from raveling, would be used to apply the pieces to the ground. After the middle of the nineteenth century, the pieces for appliqué quilts were often cut from fabrics that were of a solid color or that were printed with tiny, repetitive designs. Cardboard or tin patterns were used to mark these fabrics for cutting. A woman might make several different types of quilts, but her "best" ones were often her appliquéd quilts (Plate XIV).

The term *patchwork* was so broadly used in reference to quilting in the eighteenth century that it is impossible today to know whether it refers to pieced or appliquéd work.

Both men and women worked as professional quilters in major American cities. Sarah Powell of Philadelphia noted on June 18, 1761, that she had paid £1.11.1½ for "Callimineo, Salloon wool & Silk for a coat" and twelve shillings extra for "quilting it." Professionally produced quilting was also imported from England. For example, in the November 5, 1744, issue of the *South Carolina Gazette*, John Biswicke advertised bed blankets, bed lace, and quilts "lately imported from London."

Scraps from the ragbag were not the only sources for pieced work or appliquéd swatches. The advertisement of Jonathan and John Amory in the October 13, 1760, issue of *The Boston Evening Post* offered "English and India patches." After the Revolutionary War, American needlewomen became less dependent upon England for their printed fabrics, or "patches." The same birds and vase of flowers shown in Plate XV appear in a number of quilts. It is one of the designs produced by John Hewson, a Philadelphia calico printer.

Quilts with silk pieced tops were rarer than other types, but they were still popular throughout the eighteenth and nineteenth centuries (Figure 78). The worn areas of this quilt reveal triangular pieces of newspaper that were cut and sewn with the fab-

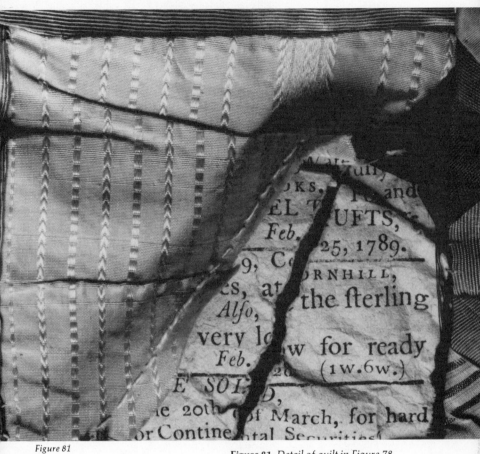

Figure 81

Figure 81. *Detail of quilt in Figure 78 showing newspapers used to stiffen the silk pieces. Newspaper dates of 1788, 1789, and 1790 can be seen in worn areas.*

Figure 82. *Brightly colored crazy quilt composed of silk scraps and ribbons fashioned into a series of fans, each of which ends in black velvet. A floral sprig, bird, or butterfly is embroidered in each section. Decorative stitching of ladder, buttonhole, cross, running, feather, satin, fern, and variations around each piece of fabric. This piece is like Figure 78 in that it is also a compendium of available fabrics for its period; but nearly one hundred years separate the two pieces. 1870–1900; H. and W. 62½"(158.75 cm); gift of Mrs. Frank H. McCormick; acc. no. 72.283.*

Figure 82

Figure 83

Figure 83. *Pieced cotton pillow cover with two tie tapes at the opening. Well-done curved piecing in the center design. All three prints are English with the predominant colors rose and tan outlined in black. Cross-stitched initials "MI" on the plain white cotton back. Originally owned by Martin Yodes of Berks County, Pa. 1820–40; H. 27⅛" (68.91 cm), W. 21⅛" (53.67 cm); acc. no. 70.270.*

ric pieces (Figure 81). It is evident that the silk-pieced quilts were being made in this manner as late as 1859, when Florence Hartley wrote *The Ladies' Hand Book of Fancy and Ornamental Work.* She advised, "In making silk patchwork, you must cut pieces of stout paper the size you wish, and baste your silk on it very carefully, and then sew them together."

Some of the most colorful and original quilts were made in the years between 1820 and 1870. Many of those surviving from that period used new fabrics selected specifically to complete the intricate designs; but many more were made by combining, in imaginative ways, scraps and patches cut from outmoded, outgrown, or worn-out garments. From this practice evolved the so-called crazy quilts that were so popular during the last quarter of the nineteenth century. The busy, haphazard designs of crazy quilts—achieved by joining many small, apparently randomly cut, pieces of material—suited perfectly the prevailing flamboyant taste of the period. Feather, chain, and ladder stitches outlined bits of silk damask, velvet, satin ribbon, and whatever else the seamstress had available (Figure 82). The patches were usually joined to their lining and interlining with coarsely spaced tufting rather than finely stitched quilting. Many of these crazy quilts were smaller than bed-size; apparently, they were intended for use as lap robes.

Quilting filled a real household need, but it also filled a social need. Pattern designs and swatches were exchanged along with gossip at the quilting party, which, on occasion, became a form of engagement announcement. Quilting parties became the female counterpart of such exclusively male activities as logrolling, "sugaring off" (boiling down maple sap), barn raising, and bullbaiting. Even today, social groups produce commemorative, or friendship, quilts, with each member contributing her patches to be combined with those of others.

Through the years, a plethora of quilting patterns has emerged. In accordance with tradition and local interpretation, a single design would be known by different names in different localities. Quilt-pattern nomenclature is therefore so chaotic that it defies orderly discussion.

Figure 84. *Appliquéd nativity scene
featuring a Georgian-style house complete
with embroidered fanlight above the door.
Angels sing and trumpet just below the
verse embroidered in outline stitch:
"Glory to God in the Highest Peace on
Earth and good will to Men Hallelujah."
Descended in the Warner family of New
York and Connecticut. Printed fabrics
used date the picture to sometime soon
after 1805; H. and W. 33½" (85.09 cm);
acc. no. 59.1496.*

Figure 84

Tambour Work

Hand-fashioned tambour work is rarely practiced today. Yet, from the last quarter of the eighteenth century until almost the mid-nineteenth century, it was one of the most fashionable needlework techniques in use (Figure 85). Paintings and prints of prominent women, such as Madame de Pompadour, sitting gracefully at their tambour frames helped to popularize tambour work as an attractive pastime.

Beginning early in the 1770s, American newspapers carried advertisements by teachers who proclaimed their ability to instruct students in this new technique. For example, the *South Carolina Gazette* (Charleston) for September 19, 1774, carried Ann Sage's notice that she would teach young ladies "Reading, Tambour, Embroidery, and all kinds of needlework." By 1800, practically every advertisement offering instruction to young ladies mentioned tambour work.

India had long been famous for the fine muslin fabrics woven there from native cotton yarns. These fabrics provided an excellent base for delicate embroidery designs, particularly those wrought with brightly colored silk yarns. For centuries, Indian workers had combined these elements to produce marvelous patterns in chain stitch worked from the fabric face with hooks instead of needles. When the technique became popular in Europe, circular frames, or hoops, were used to hold the fabric taut. The resulting drumlike appearance is what gave tambour work its name.

The basic tool used in tambour work is a tiny hook shaped much like a miniature crochet hook (Figure 86). Contemporary sources sometimes referred to it as a "shepherd's crook." One hand pushes the tambour hook through the face of the fabric, and the other hand guides yarn onto the hook from below the frame. When the hook is pulled back through the fabric, it brings a small loop above the surface. The hook advances as far as the loop permits, and then the process is repeated. An experienced tambour

Figure 85. *Tambour-decorated collar of white silk twill in pinks, greens, and yellow silk yarns. Enlarged upper detail shows that tambouring produces a chain stitch. Faint penciled lines for the design. 1815–50; H. 18″ (45.72 cm), W. 21½″ (54.61 cm); gift of Francis White; acc. no. 71.214.* **Figure 86.** *Sheer white cotton mull with tambour-worked flower sprays. The center of the larger flower has a drawn-work center. A tambour hook lies on the fabric. The hollow ivory handle holds various size hooks that may be secured in place with the set screw on the side. Fabric probably U.S.; 1790–1820; H. 107″ (271.78 cm), W. 43″ (109.22 cm); acc. no. 69.1345.*

worker could produce chain stitches much faster than a needle-worker.

Silk, metallic, linen, cotton, and even woolen yarns were used for tambour work. Although a variety of backgrounds was used, white muslin appears to have been the most favored background.

Tambour work reached its zenith around 1800, when sheer, classic, Grecian-styled dresses were decorated with delicate tambour work. By 1830, wide skirts of stiffer, heavier fabrics began to dominate fashion, and handmade tambour work fell into a decline. By the mid-1840s, machines were available to duplicate the stitch commercially. Today, machine-made white-on-white window curtains bearing tambour designs provide a reminder of a once-popular form of "fancy" needlework.

Figure 86

Knitting

Like weaving, knitting is a basic technique of textile construction. It is based on interlocking loops of yarn rather than crisscrossed yarns intersecting at right angles. Knit products have two major advantages. Their structure creates an elasticity that permits them to be stretched and then returned to their original shape; it also enables garments to be made that are virtually seamless. These two qualities make the process an ideal one for the manufacture of stockings, and for several centuries this remained the major commercial application of the process. During the American colonial period, the well-developed English knitting industry supplied quantities of knitted goods to the colonists.

In spite of its wide commercial development, knitting has remained one of the most popular of the needle arts practiced in the home. Both the tools and the technique are simple. It was therefore almost universally practiced in the early American home, particularly for making woolen stockings and mittens (Figure 87). Children—both boys and girls—as young as five or six were taught to knit. Girls often learned to knit before they learned to sew.

Stockings were a prominently visible part of the male costume in the eighteenth century. Indeed, it was the male leg that was exposed rather than the female leg. Men's stockings were often decorated with elaborate bell-like devices called clocks. Women's stockings, though presumably not visible, were usually very colorful. For a period, white stockings were considered immodest for women, although it became the most common color by the early nineteenth century. Many of these early stockings included the owner's initials in the knit, or else they were added later in cross stitch. Many stockings were numbered as well, to make it easier to pair them correctly. Professional women knitters advertised that they would repair by "new grafting and footing, all sorts of stockings."

Figure 87

Figure 87. *Left: Pillowcase with a white knitted border at one end. 1790–1840; H. 32″ (81.28 cm), W. 20″ (50.80 cm); acc. no. 67.754. Center: Finely knitted drawstring silk bag in bright shades of green, orange pink, rose, and tan; lined in dark blue silk with white polka dots. Knitted into the area just below the opening is "C: ALSOP 1817 M:A 77." Penciled on a piece of paper inside, in a 19th-century script, is "Silk Purse made by Mary Wright Alsop Great Grandmother of L. C. A. No. 84." The same woman also made the Queen's-stitched pocketbook shown in Figure 40. Middletown, Conn.; H. 6¼″ (15.87 cm), W. 3″ (7.62 cm); acc. no. 55.3.10. Right: Two pairs of white cotton miniature stockings probably used as demonstrations or for dolls. 1800–1900. Smaller pair: H. (heel to top) 2⁵⁄₁₆″ (5.86 cm), L. (toe to heel) 1⅛″ (2.87 cm); acc. no. 64.1479.1,.2. Larger pair: H. 3⅝″ (9.22 cm), L. 1¾″ (4.44 cm); acc. no. 64.1480.1,.2.*

Commercial knitting machines were operating in America by 1773, but this by no means eliminated home knitting. Perhaps as commercially produced stockings and other basic items became more readily available, women had more time to do decorative work. Lucy Alsop's silk sewing case (Figure 88) is in sharp contrast to the plain work of an earlier period. Silk yarn was usually worked in intricate patterns with very fine needles—with highly decorative results.

Cotton yarn was not widely used for knitting until after the Revolution. Then, fine denier yarns, usually white, were employed in making imitation lace edgings. These borders were popular additions to collars, pillowcases, and tablecloths throughout most of the nineteenth century (Figure 87). During the same period, whole bedspreads were also knitted in decorative designs using heavy denier yarns.

Because knitting was so common—almost an everyday occurrence—we rarely find it mentioned in contemporary letters and diaries. Knitting also played a social role, as we learn from this recollection of the year 1805 by Sarah Anna Emery in *Reminiscences of a Nonagenarian:* "It was customary for the young ladies of the neighborhood to give social tea parties of an afternoon, at which we assembled at an early hour, dressed in our best, with our go-abroad knitting work, usually of fine cotton, clocked hose. Some of these clocks comprised the most elaborate patterns. After tea the knitting was laid aside. As the evening drew on the beaux began to appear, then games, or dancing, were enjoyed."

Figure 88

Figure 88. *Knitted silk sewing case with rows of pert flowers and geometric designs done in bright greens, blues, purples, rose, and tans. "L: ALSOP" is knit in blue yarn under the flap and on the other side is "M:A • 1814." Intricately worked by Mary Alsop (see also her Figures 40 and 87) for her daughter-in-law Lucy Whittilsy Alsop. Lined with yarn-dyed, striped silk. It has three flannel half circles for needles and a pocket for a thimble and yarn. Middletown, Conn.; H. (closed) 4¼″ (10.79 cm), W. 3¾″ (9.52 cm); acc. no. 55.3.5.*

White Work

A very handsome technique, easily confused with quilting, is stuffed or corded work. Whereas quilts are constructed with an overall interlining, stuffed or corded work employs the third layer only in the design elements. Consequently, stuffed or corded work is primarily a decorative technique and is not often found in utilitarian forms such as quilts. Occasionally, however, after a piece was stuffed or corded, it was also quilted with an interlining.

A finely woven, preferably shiny, fabric was usually chosen for the top layer to emphasize the design. The bottom layer re-

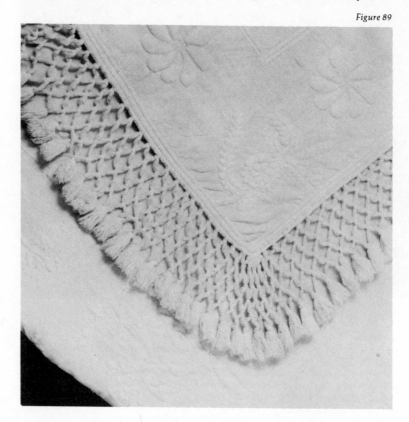

Figure 89

Figure 90

Figure 89. *Small section of a corded-work bedspread folded so that the part under the fringe shows the coarser back fabric where a little of the cording can be seen. The upper part is of very finely woven white cotton with a small portion of the designs visible. This spread bears the name "Ann Remington 1815," but is said to have been made by her sister, Mary. Mary lived in East Greenwich or Warwick, R.I., and also made the Queen's-stitched pocketbook shown in Plate V. H. 100" (254.00 cm), W. 92" (223.68 cm); acc. no. 57.67.4.* **Figure 90.** *A superbly designed and executed white stuffed-work bedspread. The urn form on the side is similar to the popular memorial monuments of the day. 1800–20; H. 87" (220.98 cm), W. 84" (213.36 cm); acc. no. 69.1705.*

Figure 91

Figure 91. *A handworked candlewicked bedspread with raised stitches created by using a tool as a gauge on a ribbed cotton ground. Probably made by the donor's great-great aunt, Mary Jane Alden Burt, who lived in Bridgewater, Conn. 1830–40; H. 113″ (287.02 cm), W. 98″ (248.92 cm); gift of Barbara Alden Hopkins Jones; acc. no. 75.113.*

quired a coarse open weave (Figure 89). The design was drawn on the back of the bottom layer, and fine running or back stitches were then worked through both fabric layers, defining the design. Next, a stiletto or similar tool was used to separate the yarns of the background fabric so that cotton wadding could be gently pushed into the outlined areas to create puffy, or "stuffed," sections. The separated fibers of the background fabric were then eased back into place. This process was usually used for creating patterns of leaves, flowers, or clusters of grapes.

Linear elements, like stems or tendrils, employed the related process of cording. With cording, after both edges of the design element were outlined by stitching, a soft bulky yarn, called *roving*, was threaded through the channels with a bodkin or large needle. Although a given piece might contain either corded or stuffed work alone, the two similar techniques are often combined.

The term *trapunto* has been used in the twentieth century to describe stuffing and cording, but it does not appear in American documents of the seventeenth, eighteenth, and early nineteenth centuries. Yet stuffing and cording were certainly well known in America from at least the late seventeenth century, especially as a means of decorating clothing. Delicate all-white coverlets (Figure 90) found much favor in early nineteenth-century America and comprise one of the most subtle yet effective applications of the technique.

Candlewick counterpanes were another part of the white-on-white phase of needlework so prominent during the first half of the nineteenth century. Candlewicking was done by machine as well as by hand. Little candlewicking is hand-embroidered today, but machine-made reproductions of earlier designs are quite popular. Machine-made designs are usually more angular and symmetrical than those embroidered by hand. A smooth, neat back is another clue to machine-made spreads; the backs of hand-embroidered candlewicking pieces are messy, with knots and yarns stretched irregularly across large areas.

Basically, candlewicking consists of fairly coarse embroidery

Figure 92

Figure 92. *Unusual use of the common sampler sentiment, "When this you see remember me when I am in eternity." The piece is signed twice: "1820 Katurah Reeve Her Work" in script on one edge, and again, in block letters, on the opposite edge. The ship in the center is impressive. The border is all in French knots; the tufts have cross-stitched backs, and diagonal satin stitch. H. 176" (447.04 cm), W. 76½" (194.31 cm); acc. no. 66.139.*

Figure 93

Figure 93. *Made in Missouri, this piece is the westernmost example in the collection. It is dated 1830, and was made by Jane Lewis Talbot, who was the step-great-grandmother of the donor. Jane, born in 1811, moved to Missouri, married, and died there in 1849. Square cotton twill ground. The unusually high tufted candlewicked design was created by closely worked small satin stitches held on top with a tool until clipped. Each of the grapes is well-rounded. H. and W. 105" (266.70 cm); gift of Charles van Ravenswaay; acc. no. 68.236.*

Figure 94

Figure 94. *Meandering vines couched with large, white, soft cotton yarns on three panels of plain-woven white ground. Other stitches are satin and bullion with a band of fringe on three sides. H. 96˝ (243.84 cm), W. 87˝ (220.98 cm); acc. no. 60.596.*

worked with soft bulky yarns on a plain-woven cotton fabric. The fabric is then washed in hot water, which shrinks it enough to lock the soft yarns in place (Figure 91). The name *candlewick* was used to describe this technique because the soft yarns incorporated resembled the cord used as wicks in early candles. A single coverlet would often contain yarn of several different diameters in order to achieve a variety of effects. These bulky yarns usually required the needlewoman to work her stitches on a fairly large scale. Outline, French knot, bullion, and satin were the most commonly used stitches (Figure 92). Tufted areas were made by looping satin or cross stitches over a spacer to create a higher pile. The loops were then cut (Figure 93). Some designs, such as grapes, were contoured by shearing the pile.

A small group of white-on-white needlework survives that used roving or candlewicking yarns to embroider designs resembling those normally found on crewel embroidery pieces. Most of this work was done on cotton or linen grounds with enlarged crewelwork stitches. When worked on a bedspread, the technique can be very attractive (Figure 94).

Less-Common Needlework Forms

Hatchments and Coats of Arms. The fact that most Americans were not entitled to a family coat of arms did not deter the more pretentious from having them. Artists, silversmiths, and professional embroiderers could be commissioned to create coats of arms—which they would do by combining various elements of coats of arms shown in heraldry books. Eleanor Purcell advertised in the *Boston Evening Post* for April 28, 1755, "Pictures and Coats of Arms embroidered on Satten." These needlework displays of pretentiousness seem to have been far more common in New England than in other areas of the colonies.

Needlework coats of arms were usually shaped to imitate hatchments—or *escutcheons*, as they were often called. A hatchment was a coat of arms, usually painted on a wooden panel within a lozenge-shaped frame, that was temporarily affixed to the front of the house when a family member died. Sometimes the hatchment was then placed in the deceased member's church. The Hall family escutcheon (Figure 95)—embroidered by a member of the Hall family—adheres to the lozenge-shape style and is probably of the type referred to by Eleanor Purcell.

One of the few surviving examples from the Philadelphia area is a small, exquisitely worked piece bearing a cipher (intertwined initials) in its lower section (Figure 97). In this piece, both silk and metallic yarns were embroidered on a cream silk moiré background.

Fewer Americans displayed coats of arms after the Revolutionary War than before it, for by then it was felt that the practice was not in keeping with republican principles. By 1800, most coats of arms had been retired to the attic.

Bed Rugs. Warm bed coverings were a necessity in the poorly heated houses of the colonial period. Quilts were used a great deal, sometimes under the body as well as over it. From this almost des-

Figure 95

Figure 95. *Satin-weave ground of black silk with embroidered arms in the traditional lozenge-shape of a hatchment. Rather coarse metallic yarns couched over padding of satin stitches. Polychrome silk yarns are finely worked in satin and outline stitches to complete the arms of the Hall family. Probably made by Hannah Hall, who was married to Thomas Fitch, a governor of Connecticut. Ca. 1730–40; H. and W. 25⅛″ (63.83 cm); acc. no. 58.1524.*

Figure 96

Figure 97

Figure 96. *The Simpkins and Symmes arms worked in
tent stitch with crewel and silk yarns. A blue
green background with the arms in shades of red,
green, yellow, blue, brown, and white. This seems
to be a fictitious crest as no arms were recorded
for Simpkins and the Symmes half displays the
crescents improperly. 1735–45; H. 20⅝" (52.40
cm), W. 18" (45.72 cm); acc. no. 57.1395.* **Figure 97.**
*Arms of the Flower Family, correctly drawn and
delicately embroidered on a small piece of cream silk
moiré ground. Satin, couching, and outline stitches
in greens, browns, and rose; silk and metallic yarns.
Old script on the back says, "Ann Flower 1763."
Pennsylvania; H. 8" (20.32 cm), W. 8½" (21.59 cm);
acc. no. 58.2226.*

perate search for warmth, it is probable that the bed rug evolved. Although today we consider rugs simply floor coverings, this was not true earlier. Noah Webster, in his 1806 *Compendious Dictionary*, defined a rug as "a rough woolen coverlet for beds." "Snug as a bug in a rug," an expression as common in the eighteenth century as it is today, takes on a somewhat more intimate connotation when considered in its original context.

The term *bed rug* occurs in the household inventories of New England and the Middle Colonies, although most such references were not to the home-embroidered types, as shown in Figure 98 and Plate XVI. The most prevalent bed rugs were commercially produced and tufted in a single color. Very few exist today because they were discarded when badly worn or out of fashion.

Figure 98

Figure 99

Figure 98. *Bed rug with coarse, two-piece linen
backing seamed down the center with looped running
stitches of multiple strands of woolen yarn.
Medium blue background with gold flowers outlined
in cream with a few accents in dark blue. Initialed
"F [E or I] B 1748"; unlined; New England; H. 88"
(223.52 cm), W. 83" (210.82 cm); acc. no. 66.605.*
Figure 99. *Sailor's suit of white linen with silk
embroidery worked in outline and satin stitches in
blue, red, beige, and green. In the early days of
the United States Navy, sailors had no regulation
uniforms and are known to have decorated their outfits
with their own embroidery. 1825–50; acc. no. 69.933.*

Figure 100

Figure 100. *This version of Liberty with
an eagle (see Figure 71) was probably
worked by a sailor. Only Liberty's face
is painted: the rest of the piece is
embroidery. Her bodice is white, her
skirt is lavender, her feet rest on
yellow ground; vivid blue water and a
mottled light blue sky are worked in outline
and satin stitches with merino yarns.
1825 – 75; H. 19¼" (48.89 cm), W. 22⅝"
(57.48 cm); acc. no. 67.893.*

Embroidered bed rugs, however, became heirlooms, and all surviving examples seem to have originated in New England. The dated bed rugs range in date from the early eighteenth century to the early nineteenth century. The form was apparently not common in other colonies, and it does not seem to have been known in England.

The needleworker almost always started bed rugs with plain-woven wool or linen backgrounds. She worked her decoration with large, multi-ply woolen yarns in a running stitch. To form a pile, she stitched uniform loops of yarn over a thin strip of wood or bone that served as a gauge.

Bed rugs are typically bold in design. Most of them suggest that their creator drew upon her crewel embroidery designs for her inspiration. Surely the extra warmth and attractiveness of these bed rugs helped to compensate for their weight.

Sailor's Embroidery. Sailors had to be adept with needle and thread in the days of the sailing ships. Sails had to be mended and clothing repaired. During off watches, needles were also used to scratch polished whalebone and ivory to make the scrimshaw articles so highly prized today.

Less well known is the fact that sailors sometimes made decorative needlework. There were no standard uniforms, and sailors embellished their clothes to suit their fancy (Figure 99). Popular prints of the day inspired the designs worked in both scrimshaw and needlework. A sailor's needlework interpretation of Liberty (Figure 100), worked in merino yarns, makes an interesting contrast with the more refined Liberty worked in silk and spangles (Figure 71).

Documented examples of American marine embroidery are rare; many more embroideries are known to have been done on British vessels.

Selected Bibliography

Andere, Mary. *Old Needlework Boxes and Tools*. Devon: David & Charles, Ltd., 1971.

Baker, Muriel L. *The ABC's of Canvas Embroidery*. Sturbridge: Old Sturbridge Village, Inc., 1968.

————. *A Handbook of American Crewel Embroidery*. Rutland: Charles E. Tuttle Co., 1966.

Bolton, Ethel Stanwood and Coe, Eva Johnston. *American Samplers*. 1921. Princeton: Pyne Press, 1973.

Caulfield, S. F. H. and Saward, Blanche C. *The Dictionary of Needlework*. 1882. New York: Arno Press, Inc., 1972.

Colby, Averil. *Quilting*. New York: Charles Scribner's Sons, 1973.

Cooper, Grace Rogers. *The Copp Family Textiles*. Washington, D. C.: Smithsonian Institution Press, 1971.

Davidson, Ruth Bradbury. *Concise Encyclopedia of American Antiques*. Edited by Helen Comstock. New York: Hawthorn Books, 1958.

Davis, Mildred. *The Art of Crewel Embroidery*. New York: Crown Publishers, Inc., 1962.

————. *Early American Embroidery Designs*. New York: Crown Publishers, Inc., 1969.

Everett, Ethel Walton. "Studies in Stitchery." *Antiques* (June 1939) 39: 284–87.

Garrett, Elisabeth Donaghy. "American Samplers and Needlework Pictures: Part I: 1739–1806." *Antiques* (February 1974) 105: 356–64; "Part II: 1806–1840" (April 1975) 107: 688–701.

Ginsburg, Cora. "Textiles in the Connecticut Historical Society." *Antiques* (April 1975) 107: 712–25.

Groves, Sylvia. *Needlework Tools and the History of Accessories.* London: Country Life, Ltd., 1966.

Grow, Judith K. and McGrail, Elizabeth C. *Creating Historic Samplers.* Princeton: Pyne Press, 1974.

Harbeson, Georgiana Brown. *American Needlework.* New York: Crown Publishers, Inc., 1938.

Hedlund, Catherine A. *A Primer of New England Crewel Embroidery.* Sturbridge: Old Sturbridge Village, Inc., 1963.

Homer, Marianna Merritt. *The Story of Samplers.* Philadelphia: Philadelphia Museum of Art, 1971.

Howe, Margery Burnham. *Early American Embroideries in Deerfield.* Deerfield: Heritage Foundation, 1963.

Hughes, Therle. *English Domestic Needlework 1660–1860.* London: Abby Fine Arts, 1961.

Landon, Mary Taylor and Swan, Susan Burrows. *American Crewelwork.* New York: The Macmillan Co., 1970.

Lane, Rose Wilder. *Woman's Day Book of American Needlework.* New York: Simon and Schuster, 1963.

Levey, Santina. *Discovering Embroidery of the Nineteenth Century.* Tring, Herts: Shire Publications, n.d.

Orlofsky, Patsy and Myron. *Quilts in America.* New York: McGraw-Hill Book Co., 1974.

Peto, Florence. *American Quilts and Coverlets.* New York: Chanticleer Press, 1949.

Ring, Betty. "The Balch School in Providence, Rhode Island." *Antiques* (April 1975) 107: 660–70.

———. "Collecting American Samplers Today." *Antiques* (June 1972) 101: 1012–18.

Rowe, Ann Pollard. "Crewel Embroidered Bed Hangings in Old and New England." *Boston Museum Bulletin* (1973) 71: 101–66.

Safford, Carleton L. and Bishop, Robert. *America's Quilts and Coverlets.* New York: E. P. Dutton & Co., Inc., 1972.

Schiffer, Margaret B. *Historical Needlework of Pennsylvania.* New York: Charles Scribner's Sons, 1968.

Swain, Margaret H. *Historical Needlework: A Study of Influences in Scotland and Northern England.* New York: Charles Scribner's Sons, 1970.

Swan, Susan B. "Worked Pocketbooks." *Antiques* (February 1975) 107: 298–303.

Vanderpoel, Emily Noyes. *American Lace & Lace-Makers.* Edited by Elizabeth C. Barney Buel. New Haven: Yale University Press, 1924.

Wardle, Patricia. *Guide to English Embroidery.* London: Her Majesty's Stationery Office, 1970.